THE WRITE 2 HEAL

It's Not About the Sight Lost, but Vision Gained

JEANETTA PRICE

with co-authors Jasmin Duffey, Lynette Eberhardt, Samuel Jonita Gates, Stacie Leap, Daria Bannerman, Kamille Richardson Krystle Allen, Cheryl Minnette, Mirranda Williams

Phoenix Publishing House, LLC
Publishers since 2016
P. O. BOX 154855
Lufkin, TX 75904

www.phoenixpubllc.com

Printed in the United States of America

ISBN: 978-1-955235-10-5

DEDICATION

To whom

That sits in a dark room

Afraid of the unknown

A stranger in your own home

Please know that you are not alone

Despite what you might see

Never be fooled by challenges that be

Because you hold the key

To be free

"It's not about the sight lost, but vision gained."

Jeanetta Price

DISCLAIMER

This book is an Anthology. It reflects the authors' present recollections of experiences over time. Some names and characteristics have been changed, some events have been compressed, and some dialogue has been recreated.

CONTENT TRIGGER WARNING

This book includes recounts of domestic and physical violence. We acknowledge that this content may be difficult. We also encourage you to care for your safety and well-being.

Table of Contents

Table of Contents

ACKNOWLEDGMENT

I would like to acknowledge life, and every riddle along the way that I could not solve which drew me closer to God. I am extremely grateful for my family, friends, and colleagues who supported the vision of the book.

A special thank you to Magdeline Giron at Eye Centers of Southeast Texas who nursed me with prayers during each procedure and the late Dr. Richard A. Levacy, who cared for my eyes as if they were his own. I am forever in debt to my “Vision Dream Team” of doctors at Baylor College of Medicine, and it was truly love at first “contact” when I met Dr. Keith Manuel.

I cannot express enough thanks to Texas Workforce Commission Vocational Rehabilitation Services. Since my humble beginnings as a newly blind individual, the agency has served as a vital component of my overall growth, employment, and educational success.

I must express my gratitude to the National Federation of the Blind for the opportunity to witness the power of blind visionaries who helped shape and mold me to the leader I am today.

I am sincerely grateful for my fifth-grade teacher, Ms. Wanda Mattarocci, who was the first person to acknowledge my God given gifts of writing and acting.

Ms. Mattarocci placed me in my first stage play, and now I write plays.

I am immensely thankful for Phoenix Publishing and the OUTTA SIGHT Co-Authors who labored countless hours, and never lost sight of the vision.

Last but not least, I would like to acknowledge my belated father, Cornell Price II, who loved me unconditionally and believed that his baby girl did no wrong.

Introduction

The Heart of a Writer

I write my way out of hard times. I write my way while having good times. I write to release pain, not intending to gain fame or likes. I write to express what I suppress. I write what I hide, so you must read between the lines. I write with no limitations, excuses, or lies. I write what I see beyond the eyes. I write with the love of the spoken words. I write with freedom of creativity, not searching for the right verbs. My words are action—directly aligned with my vision.

It's my season to write! I am on a mission of healing others and being healed through sharing my test! Mic check this out! I'm an undercover ghostwriter behind the scenes; there is no need to be seen. I write how I walk independently! I write without paper or pen. I write with my soul, blood, sweat, and tears. As I recite, I get chills. I write with fire because I'm a survivor. I write. Alright, I'm guilty of that crime. Sentence me to life. You cannot lock me down. My spoken words travel from cell to cell. Tried to defeat me but failed! You have no power. I am the child of The Most-High. He has blessed me with the gift of writing. As long as I have breath, I shall write. Writing is my life support. Can you feel it? My heart beats with the rhythm of the ink. Can you hear it? That's the sound of a writer's heart. Come a little closer. Read the closed caption. You have the "Write 2 Heal."

Wait a Minute!

We must pray before we get this party started! I am sincerely sorry, but I got it from my mama. She would not crank up the car until we prayed. I recall mama motionless in the driver seat of the unattractive, diesel sounding, pimple face body, midnight blue four-door vehicle that was the length of a limousine in which we called a "hooptie." I often daydreamed in the back seat about riding in the front seat of the hooptie, waving at my fans (older siblings) as if I was Miss America.

I wonder if Miss America had to sit in the back seat of the hooptie because she was the youngest sibling. I would never get a chance to recline in the front while teasing the old-school fans in the back. That sounds like sweet revenge to me! Meanwhile, I continued to slump in my appointed position, the back seat. All passengers in the hooptie stopped breathing as my mother carefully examined her prey while contemplating which one would deliver the prayer.

Suddenly, a fishwife voice growled, "Jeanetta, lead the prayer."

In my head, but I dared not to announce, "Why me again?"

As politely as I could muster in my sweetest tone, I replied, "Yes, ma'am. Everyone, please bow your heads."

My stomach was in knots as I attempted to pull together a prayer that would not only give us safe passage to our destination but also get our hooptie to start. Once I was done, we all inhaled as mama cranked the car. After several failed attempts, it would finally start giving us a relief to exhale. Won't He do it!

I would like to offer a similar prayer of protection for you as you journey through the triumphant stories of the authors within these pages.

Dear Heavenly Father,

We humbly ask that You protect us as we travel to a place of healing. Let no harm or danger enter our paths. Anoint every word written and allow it to be a blessing to the passengers. God, we ask that you remove the spirit of fear and replace it with radical faith that one will receive their healing. We decree and declare healing, renewal of the mind, and a breakthrough from any strongholds in Jesus Christ's name. Amen!

All aboard as you experience our Write 2 Heal!

Jeanetta Price

Beautifully Healed

Being the youngest and biggest sibling was a little challenging at times. My older sisters, Khat and Shan, also known as "The Banks Girls," were jealous because they weren't this fine. All I can say is favor ain't fair, sis! Most people thought that my sisters were twins because they looked so much alike. Plus, they were born in the same year. What can I say? My mother was busy in 1973.

That reminds me, I used to tell all my sisters' business. For this reason, I often had to advocate for myself by utilizing my immense bold vocals singing, "Mama, help!" They proceeded to chase me around the projects with banana peelings. It was the slimy texture for me. Don't judge me! Anyway, I continued to tell all their business, and I paid dearly for my actions.

However, they paid dearly for their actions too.Trust me; the whole house received a whipping if I received a whipping. Afterward, The Banks Girls would call me names such as "Spoiled Brat, Drama Queen, and Big Baby." My siblings will all agree today that I am a forty-three-year-old baby who is PHAT(Praiseworthy-Honorable-Amazing-Trailblazer). See, they really love me in their own toxic way. Smooches!

On the other hand, my one and only brother Cornell, also known as Poodie, served as my protector and tolerated me somewhat better. The only thing was that he was the ultimate hustler growing up, and I served as his number one hustle. For example, he hustled me into eating his vegetables and washing his dishes. Oh, I can't forget that I was his watch girl when stealing mama's hooptie for a night out of enjoyment. Of course, Poodie had to pay me some hush money. All I can say is the price is right, even when we are wrong! No worries. He always found a way to hustle back.

When mama was missing in action, the siblings would play. "Attention, fans! Are you ready for some wrestling?" One of us would yell out to an imaginary stand filled with people. Well, wrestling night was a match between the siblings. It would be the Banks against the Prices. It really wasn't any competition. The Banks demolished us for years until Poodie woke up around the seventh grade and had grown muscles overnight. That's right! My brother had been drinking milk, and hard work paid off. Then the tables turned on wrestling night. We gained a couple of wins under our belt, and we finally earned some *respect* around the house.

Seriously, how much respect can you expect with nicknames like Poodie and Moo-Moo? Yes, we were cursed by being initiated into a family where the elders gave us a nickname. For instance, Brickhouse is more like a brick mansion today. Welcome to Big Girl City, little cousin.

We have Cousin Tanna Boo, Little Toe, and Big Toe with the freckles. Big Toe and I was born a day apart. I demanded that he put some respect on my name as the older cousin by addressing me with a handle—Miss Price. Oh, Snaps! I dare not forget about Cousin Fifty AKA Lucy because she looked and acted like an old lady since she was a child. However, Uncle Perry gave my brother the nickname Poodie.

One day, I asked Uncle Perry, "What is a Poodie?" He burst with laughter and replied, "A Poodie is a little boy with a big forehead." Eventually, Poodie grew into his forehead, but his nickname has traveled with him throughout life. Well, I can thank my beautiful mother for gifting me with the nickname Moo-Moo. Most people call me Moo for short. Mother said I was the only child who came out cornbread fed, so she thought calling me her little Moo-Moo was cute.

I tried my best to keep my nickname on the down-low, but I come from a family of big mouths, so all you heard was "Mooooo!"

I was not bad but adventurous and had a high

risk for accidents. Around the age of five, Poodie and I were jumping in bed. It was raining, so we entertained ourselves by jumping from the dresser to the bed, practicing our wrestling moves.

On the dresser sat a large dill pickle jar full of marbles. Until this day, I am not sure how I jumped off the dresser and ended up on the floor on top of the shattered pickle jar with marbles rolling in a puddle of my blood. Poodie took cover by hiding under the bed when Mama entered the room like a bolt of lightning while shouting, "Mooo!" Mother did not wait on 911. Instead, she zoomed me to the emergency room right on time. The doctor disclosed that I was lucky because the glass was extremely close to my spine, so I could have been paralyzed. However, the outcome was minor—a total of forty-eight stitches and light-duty, more like no play. He must have been crazy!

The same week, I went outside, not to play but to grab some fresh air, and managed to smother a bed of ants with my buttocks. I leaped up like it was fire shut up in my bottom. I ran home screaming at the top of my lungs. Mom met me on the porch and beat those ants off me with my clothes. The entire projects witnessed me in my birthday suit.

Afterward, mom marinated me with some of that greenish alcohol and dared me to move off the couch while she finished frying fish. It wasn't over. I topped the day off by choking on a fishbone. Mom beat my back like she was Ike Turner, but I was not forced to eat the cake. However, it felt like she made me eat a whole loaf of bread and drank a gallon of milk before that fishbone went down. At that point, I wished for better days ahead, and I dismissed myself to bed.

Ask and ye shall receive. "Go, Moo! Go, Moo!" That's all you heard at our high school pep rallies. I had the most spirit in the class of 1996. I was a big girl but light on my feet. I was the most confident and only plus-size figure out of all my friends. I got in good trouble with my partner in crime, my stepsister, Denise, but I lovingly call her Bonaisha because she has split personalities that often got us in more trouble.

Unexpectedly, my weight plummeted one hundred pounds in addition to my hair falling out, dry skin, and low energy. My mom required me to sleep with her at night due to fear that I would stop breathing. I felt sorry for my mother because she had restless nights to prevent me from slipping away in my sleep. I remember we were scheduled to see the third doctor, praying that he had a clue as to what was going on with me.

Due to experience, he was clueless and attempted the same protocol as the prior physicians, such as pregnancy and HIV testing based on statistics. I was a virgin, not a statistic. I was convinced that my destiny was an early casket.

Knock!

Knock!

Who's there?

Death.

Well, come on in.

Have a seat.

Don't you think it's a little too early that we meet?

In the future, no surprises by banging on the back door.

Enter through the front; I am not afraid of you anymore.

Expose yourself as the thief you are.

So I can warn others near and far.

To prepare for unwanted guest who is out to still one's joy.

Mom and I sat hopelessly in the doctor's office. I leaned my head on her shoulder as a gentle tear rolled down my face unto my lips; I could taste the bitterness of fear. Finally, the nurse called us to the back to go over my labs which all came back negative. That would be considered strike three, back to square one.

Hold up. It's a foul ball! Oh my God! We are back in the game. A lovely woman encouraged my mom to take me to John Sealy's Children's Hospital in Galveston, Texas. We deserted our home with new faith the next day, searching for my healing.

When I entered the hospital's doors, I felt a sense of comfort. I realized that this place was hope for sick children like me. The staff was incredibly supportive and encouraging.

I saw a twinkle in my mother's eyes, and I knew I was going to be alright. We did not prepare for a staycation of thirty days, so the nurses promised mom they would take care of me as she returned home before it got too late.

A couple of weeks passed, and my "get up and go" returned. Plus, the doctor found a solution to treat my thyroid condition. The next day, I received radiation treatment to shrink the thyroid. I was released from inpatient care with doctor's orders that sentenced me to thirty days at home. Jesus healed me! Now back to the regular program. Go Moo! Go Moo!

Chow Time

As I lay on the surgery table, stretched out like a piece of meat seasoned and stuffed with fear, ready to be smoked on the pit from hell, you smell my nerves as the aroma drifted throughout the room as the enemy sat anxiously to have a feast as if I was deceased.

In 1999, I was in the midst of a horrific storm. Within the blink of an eye, the sky grew dark gray. The angry clouds were trapped with fear because the presence of death was near.

The raging winds overpowered my ability, knocking me off my feet over and over again, marking my space. I was hell-bound. Deadly raindrops murdered my spirit with sinful acts of guilt and shame because I could not recall the last time I called out the name Jesus!

I was twenty-one, honey-blonde hair, grown woman curves, checking account looking nice, new wardrobe and car. I was high on life! I went from working all week to partying all weekend.

As a matter of fact, I was at the club drinking ice-cold beer and jamming to that Southside. On my way home from the club, I knew that I was not going to make it home. I pulled under the underpass and crumpled over the steering wheel. By this time, the pain was excruciating. It felt like lighting and thundering beating me unmercifully in my head. Then I heard a wicked voice.

"Girl, I am not the one to gossip, but I heard you're going to die. It is not bragging, but I just

smashed a vessel in your brain. I felt a need to introduce myself before I took you out. My name is Aneurysm, but all my friends call me Ann. Did I interrupt your little storyline? My bad. Hurry up. Your time is running out."

In the midst, I heard my mama say, "Baby, there is power in His name," and I took all that I had and cried out His name. "*Jesus*!" He gave me the strength to keep pressing on the gas pedal.

Every time I felt I could not go anymore, I heard His calming voice, "Keep pressing, my child."

During my eight-hour brain surgery, "Keep pressing."

The doctor said I wasn't going to walk and talk. "Keep pressing."

I had another thirty-day staycation at John Sealy Hospital. Unfortunately, my local hospital was not equipped to conduct life-threatening surgery. For this reason, I was returned to my main man, old faithful John, to receive my healing.

One time for the birthday girl! Hello, twenty-five! Excuse me. I meant twenty-FINE! I must admit; life had been treating a sista' right. I was in love with a handsome brother that looked like LL Cool J, but I called him "Butterfinger." I know how Beyonce felt crazy in love, and I was all the above. What else could happen to me? I am finally seeing better days. I had survived several storms of life. I was for sure that this was my rainbow season. The keyword was *rain*, and when it rains, it floods where I come from.

The next storm in my life I did not see coming, and it literally blinded me.

"Why is my computer screen fuzzy?" I shifted in my chair, rubbing my eyes, wondering if the stress and long hours of the impending storm was getting to me. The hospital is overcrowded with patients and staff in a panic because a hurricane is predicted to land soon. I was assigning beds as fast as possible, and my eyes were extremely irritated from looking at this screen all day.

Suddenly, I felt needles stabbing the sight out of my left eye. I attempted to focus by feeling my way around my office like a blind woman. Who? Not me! "Jeanetta, just breathe and log off your computer. Lord!" I gasp for air while crying out in a moan.

My supervisor led me to the hospital clinic. The doctor examined my eye and referred me to a local specialist. I drove myself to the specialist who referred me to the surgeon, Dr. Levacy. By the time I made it, I was a nervous wreck, and so was his staff when they realized I drove myself. Yes, you read right. I drove myself! I parked my car diagonally and dared someone to say something! I rushed through the center's doors with urgency. The staff sent me directly to the back.

Dr. Levacy entered with a peaceful spirit to calm Hurricane Jeanetta! He explained that a blister was covering my left eye and needed a transplant due to an eye condition called Keratoconus. The nurse explained the procedure, and I was in surgery within a week.

The corneal transplant consisted of donor tissue that blessed me to see again. A stranger donated their sight to me. How unselfish. I foolishly said proudly, "They will bury me with all my organs." My feelings have drastically changed since that day. I have one question. Have you ever eaten humble pie?

Now, the fight for my sight is on! About a week in the game, the corneal transplant was rejected. I was back in surgery, but I was introduced to aggressive glaucoma this time. I lost my job, confidence, and Butterfinger. But losing him was a gain! I struggled with depression and thoughts of suicide. There were a total of twenty-two eye procedures, and my sight was diminishing along with my will to live.

I felt no one in my family understood my pain, especially my mother, who expressed how ungrateful I was to be worried about some old eyes when God had delivered me from a brain aneurysm.

I often wonder why God saved me from a brain

aneurysm to take my sight. They say He doesn't make no mistakes! I was always told that God blessed me with a gift to write. In that season, I gave it back to him, and I refused to write. Why write when I can't see? I can't drive! I can't work! I can't live like this!

Four dark years passed by, and finally, the state confirmed that I was blind enough to receive benefits from Vocational Rehabilitation Services. Woo-hoo! Was I supposed to be happy? I had lost everything due to blindness. I would skip doctor visits to save for the next visit because I had no insurance. Dr. Levacy continued to see me and cleared my debt. He encouraged me not to give up on my sight because technology was advancing daily.

Unfortunately, Dr. Levacy could no longer care for my eyes and referred me to his partner in healing, Dr. Marshall B. Hamill. Years passed. Beauty faded. I felt like the ugly blind cow! I no longer desired to be amongst the living. Please take me out of my misery!

I did not accept that I was a blind woman. My sunglasses blocked the curious stares due to the distortion of my left eye. A total of twenty-two eye procedures were all in vain. I had the right to have a pity party. Amid my pity party, I heard the Holy Spirit again. "Keep pressing." Something got all over me! This time, it wasn't no ants. It was a burning sensation shut up in my bones. I sprang out of that bed, almost touching the ceiling. It was like an epiphany.

My vision was the third eye that Aunt Henny mentioned to me as a child. Well Chicken Thunder! I entertained Aunt Henny with my writings growing up, and she stated that I was wise before my years. OMG! I must *Write 2 Heal*! I will write my way out of depression. I will write OUTTA SIGHT! I was literally walking blind, but today I rise! I laid here for four years too long, sleeping in a bed of depression, acting like my life was over. God forgive me! I was angry at my family, friends, and everybody in between, which held me hostage for years.

I began to pray as if it was my last prayer, and I received confirmation. "Keep pressing." So I pressed myself to write daily. Even though I could barely see the paper, I continued to write. I purchased different color sharpies and notebooks. My senses did not heighten, but my creativity flourished. I began to write what I was feeling, no longer filled with bitterness but love. Not only do I write for my healing, but I have been blessed to write other people's truth, such as my mother. She was physically and sexually abused in the home as a child.

I'm writing for you, Mama! I write for every untold story! I *Write 2 Heal*! Finally, I realized that it is not about the sight lost but vision gained.

With this newfound confidence, I decided to go get everything God set forth for me. I went back to college, receiving my bachelor's in social work and a master's in counseling.

I recall my first year in the counseling program. My professor strongly encouraged me to discontinue the program because she had never seen a blind counselor. I passed my state board on December 16, 2020. Won't He keep doing it! Do you see a blind counselor now? That same professor became my mentor and good friend. She admitted that she was blind, and I was the one with the vision.

"Are You Blind?"

Are you blind? That's the question at hand. Before they even shake my hand, it's the only thing they see, and I assure you it's not me. Of course, it is my blindness!

"Excuse me, ma'am, you don't look blind."

Well, could you please explain to me how blindness looks? See, blindness is not the presenting problem. Instead, the lack of knowledge and misconceptions of blindness serves as society's blindfolds. Low expectations create social barriers that prevent us from reaching our goals.

"Why you walk with that stick?" That is the question. Correction this is not, nor will it ever be, a stick. It is my cane. In the blind community, we name our canes. Please show some love for my bestie. She never leaves my side. As a matter of fact, she's my eyes. I walk with Faith into a world of possibilities believing that I can tap into my vision.

Faith detects roadblocks, allowing me to overcome life's obstacles, change direction, and discover the impossible.

"Are you blind?" That is the question at hand before they even shake my hand. Are you blind? Yes. Once I finally said it with no shame, I took back my name—Jeanetta Price, and I'm blind.

That's when I "real-eyes" that the question all this time was not for me but for you, who have sight but no vision. Are you blind?

I was so afraid of blindness because of the misconceptions and stereotypes. There was a time when you could not say Jeanetta and blind in the same breath. I would be ready to two-piece you. But trust me, I am still under construction.

Fast forward, I am the founder and CEO of an inspirational company, Blind Girl Magic (BGM), but it's the vision for me. BGM spreads awareness of the positive aspect of blindness by tapping into our arts of poetry, monologues, plays, music, and the list goes on. Reflecting on my life, each test of life is my testimony today.

Praise report time! About four years ago, I received a unique contact called scleral lens from an Ophthalmologist, Dr. Manuel. Of course, I gave Dr. Hamill the side-eye, but I was obedient, so I cautiously proceeded forward with his referral.

"Wow!" I informed the doctor that I could see his face. That's when he told me to look at mine. "Well, I declare. My wig was crooked, and nobody told me!" I begin to laugh as well as cry.

I asked the doctor if I could look at the sky, which was priceless! I only can see light perception in my left eye, but that right eye went from 20/400 visual acuity to 20/40 with that contact. Won't He continue to do it? Finally, I could renew my license and buy a car after fifteen years. I had never been so proud to be so wrong. I thought my life was over. Yes, the price was wrong! Did I just say that? Please don't tell nobody. I'll eat your vegetables. Go Moo! Go Moo!

And she lives happily ever after. Right? Wrong. Allow me to explain. Once you arrive at a healing place, you must continue practicing your healing techniques for the simple fact that the enemy waits for an opportunity to steal your joy.

I had been blessed to experience sight again. So why am I feeling depressed now? I encountered rejection, envy, and jealousy from the blind and sighted community. I begin to look in the mirror and tell myself, "You are so ugly." I hated my dark, dry skin, double chin, and left eye, which captured unwanted attention. What was given as a blessing, I felt was a curse. No one expected me to be in this place.

I walked around with a mask pretending to be all people expected me to be. I had no desire to live. "God,

I'm ready if it's Your will."

To be known for your high spirit and over-the-top personality, it's easy for others to be blinded from the truth. But one day, the dark shades were removed, and my truth was revealed. I was staring in the mirror, feeding my soul words of self-hate and negativity. I was abruptly interrupted by my sister by love, Rikesha.

With boldness, she demanded, "Stop!" We locked eyes. It appeared that she was speaking to my soul. "Stop it!" She continued, "You will not pick on yourself since you got this little contact!" I cried out of shame that my insecurities had been exposed. Kesha reminded me that I was beautiful and loved. On that day, I picked up my pen to WRITE 2 Heal again in the most "Beautiful" way.

Beautifully Healed

I hate the whips that's imbedded within my skin from stretching. Or how I wear my hair over my eye. Y'all think I'm so fly but it's to hide the disfiguration of my eye. "Weight!" I refuse to stand, afraid it's going to reveal the truth that I am not prepared to face. So I hide behind a mask praying that you don't see my wide backside, double chin, or imperfect smile that frowns upon a chipped tooth. Because I have been taught that this was so unattractive, I unconsciously place one hand over my mouth when I am laughing. Insecurities bruises you internally. Perfect Patty is who I'll never be!

All the kids use to tease me, “get away from me with your Big Bubble lips!” And when I looked in the mirror it disgusted me; I saw ugly as I replayed the voices of girls making fun of my nappy hair, large Nose, and even my clothes, clueless that they were killing me softly with their words. So Powerful the tongue can be known as the pink tornado. It destroyed my self-esteem and it did not help that I was the biggest child on the team, lagging behind shame, afraid to come out the dressing room, so I’d cry!!

Praying that the tears would roll off my dark completion so I could be a lighter version and the boys might like me, might even say hi to me! Oh how I wished I looked like Barbie! Pointed Nose! Vanilla skin! Thin! Did I mention thin? Thin like anorexia, thin like bulimia who has caused a million little girls as well as women to slit their wrist or end up mentally impaired because they are dying to fit in society’s image of beautifully thin! The thin Line between love and hate. Insecurity seeds are known to be planted in one’s childhood grows into adolescent and harvest in adulthood. Insecurities bruise you internally leaving open wounds that only He can heal.

Lord, I believe it and receive it in Your Name! Insecurities no longer define me! I am who my father created me to be Beautifully Healed!

Jasmin Duffey

Benched Not Broken

I remember sitting and wondering why bad things would happen to good people and why bad people seemed to be the ones blossoming in life. As a child, my relationship with God was not my own. I was instructed how to believe in God and how He operated, and with those instructions, I understood that I should never question God… so I didn't. Now, there I was, very young, and my mind still so innocent and easily controlled that it left me in turmoil.

Now you do the math. A curious child with questions minus someone to ask them equals a dangerous mind. I would think things like, maybe I was such a terrible person in my past life that God decided to punish me in this one, or perhaps I'm paying for someone else's karma.

Even at a young age, I understood how someone's karma could directly affect them without directly affecting them. Maybe I was being punished for not always listening to my parents. Secretly I thought Santa was the one who punished me for that, not God. I didn't know. I did see that it was something about the story of Job from the Bible that always tugged at me. I started to think that if I just stayed strong through everything I went through and never questioned God in the process, I would be blessed like Job.

Before I really open up and give you all a glimpse into my world, allow me to introduce myself. My name is Jasmine Duffey. Well, really, it's spelled *Jasmin.* There is a funny story about how I misspelled it for years. A long-running joke was that either I was switched at birth or that my mom was in so much pain from having to push out a nine-pound thirteen-ounce, twenty-three-inch baby that she forgot to add the E. I found out the proper spelling of my name when I was sixteen years old at the DMV, trying to get my license.

I vividly remember how I argued the lady at the counter down. Then after having my birth certificate held in my face by a stranger to show me I was wrong, I started to believe all those times my siblings bullied me and told me I was adopted and that I was the milk man's baby. Then I found out that both of my sisters also went through similar situations. I concluded that either we were switched at birth, we all were adopted, or nobody paid attention to birth certificates back then.

I was born and raised in Jonesboro, Georgia. Still, my younger years were spent going back and forth from Georgia, where my father is from, and Mobile, Alabama, where my mother is from.

My childhood nicknames were Fiji, which came from my Aunt Cint. My mother's sister said I was named after a female wrestler who beat everybody up. My other nickname is Scooter. According to my family, it came from the fact that I was always on the go. I definitely fit the description of what some would consider a tomboy, although if you ask me, I beg to differ.

I don't think I'm a tomboy at all. I just like to think of myself as a girl that likes to do boy things. I mean, why should the boys get to have all the fun? I was that little girl on the playground wearing a dress and hair bows playing baseball and football with the boys. Dolls never seemed appealing to me. I hated hair bows, and wearing dresses felt like capital punishment.

I'm the daughter of two amazing parents, Alvin and Joann Duffey, and the sister to the dopest siblings in the world, Jovonda, Jawanda, Jarvis, and Janitris.

My parents met at Clark Atlanta University, where they played basketball on full scholarships. The word on the street is that both of my parents dominated the court! As you can guess, two athletes would come together to create an amazing superstar like myself.

My sister Vonda was like a little version of my mom growing up. She did my homework for me. I mean, she helped me with my homework, got me up and dressed for school, and walked me to the school bus.

My brother was the one I played sports and video games with. My little sister was and still is my little mini-me. Although Janitris didn't grow up with us, it felt like she was always there when she did come back into our lives.

Now that we are no longer strangers, I feel more comfortable letting you into my space. I think it's important to mention that my dad stands at six foot ten, and my mother at six foot three, so as you probably guessed, I too am a giant standing at six foot seven. Now, I'm not bragging. Although height is a beautiful thing, I am telling you this because height played a significant part in many things that changed the course of my life.

Let me explain. At the early age of three, my parents noticed that I had problems with my vision. I would get extremely close to the TV, and when I did things such as coloring or practice writing my name, I would get so close to the paper that they said it looked as though I was trying to eat it.

My parents immediately took me to the doctor, thinking that a cute pair of glasses would be a simple fix. Yet to their dismay, it was found that I was growing too fast. The muscles in my eyes were developing more quickly than the rest of my body. This caused the lenses in my eyes to be dislocated, which would explain why I couldn't see! In addition, the focus of everything I was looking at was off.

Surgery was the only option, so surgery it was. I went in to get the lenses in my eyes completely removed. That surgery fixed one issue but created a whole different problem. When you get the lens in your eyes removed, you have two choices after that. You can either wear contacts to replace the lens removed or wear glasses. My parents tried the contacts first, but I want you to stop at this moment and think about any three-year-old kid in your life. I'll wait. Okay, now imagine having to hold that three-year-old down every day while trying to put some contacts in their eyes.

Y'all, I acted a fool. Picture this. My dad tried his best to hold down my legs, which were kicking for dear life, by the way, my sister holding down one of my arms, my brother holding down the other arm, and my mother holding my face while trying to put a contact in my eye. All this came after they had to come to find me hiding under the bed. Luckily for them, we didn't have all these cameras everywhere as we do now. I know that people would've sworn that my parents were abusing me.

So that lasted about a good month. Then my parents decided to go with the glasses. Now here is where the other problem became a factor. These weren't just regular glasses. They were bifocals that were literally in my mind the size of the outer mirrors on a car. To add insult to injury, they were bright pink. Now, don't get me wrong, when I put them on, I could see to the moon and back. But I didn't want to wear them because the kids bullied me so badly. Kids that young shouldn't even know what bullying is. However, they definitely did. So even though I was young, I still developed insecurities that, unfortunately, have followed me into adulthood.

Moving on, I'm not quite sure how we were introduced to Ben Hill Recreation Center. Still, that place played a significant part in making me the person I am today. It was there I met my first love. My parents, just like most parents, put my siblings and me in several activities to see what we would grow a liking to.

First, they put me in a dance class. I hated it. They made me cheer, and I cried every time I saw a pom pom. Next, they made me try tennis. Boy, stop. Softball wasn't that bad, but it was the heat for me. Then they put a basketball in my hand, and I instantly fell in love. I'm not talking about no puppy love. I'm talking about the type of love that once you experience it, you crave it to the point that it almost becomes a drug for you.

Due to me being so young, my parents unknowingly ignored my talent at first. It wasn't until Mr. Walker, the gym owner, approached my dad and told him that he needed to immediately sign me up to start playing competitive basketball because he could see the potential in me.

They did, and I loved every second of it. Unfortunately, my parents still made me dance and cheer, but I would always get in trouble for sneaking out of dance class to go to the gym. It took a while, but eventually, they caught the hint and let me just play ball.

Unfortunately, there wasn't a girls' team for me

to play on, so there I was, the only girl on an all-boys team, and I was dominating. I'm sure all the boys hated it! At age ten, I started playing on an all-girls team, which my dad coached. I ended up playing with those same group of girls up until my tenth-grade year. After that, I played ball in school, but all my summers were spent playing with these girls at Ben Hill.

Let's fast forward to the age of thirteen, when my height would once again become an issue. This was around the time that I hit an extreme growth spurt that my body could not handle. I shot up so fast that my bones couldn't keep up, so they became fragile. One day, while playing summer league ball, I went for the ball, collided with another player, and tore my ACL. I had surgery and had to sit out for a few months, but that wasn't even the worse part of it.

The worst part after having surgery was not playing ball and doing physical therapy. I tore the ACL in my other knee in my first game back. Usually, this would break somebody, right? I mean, maybe someone with weak bones shouldn't be playing competitive sports. I didn't care. I loved basketball so much that I worked twice as hard in physical therapy to bounce back faster. I recovered so quickly that even the doctors couldn't believe it.

Fast forward, I'm in high school. My parents finally trusted me to begin wearing contacts again. The glasses were gone. My knees were healed, and I was ready to really start making a name for myself. I walked in as a freshman at Jonesboro High School. I earned my spot as a starter on the varsity basketball team, which opened the flood gates to college recruiters. I remember playing in games where there were at least fifty recruiters in the crowd at one time. I was a freshman and deciding what college I wanted to attend was the last thing on my mind.

One day while I was in the gym, the volleyball team coach approached me and asked if I would play for his team. I had never played a volleyball game a day in my life, nor was I interested. But he was an amazing coach.

Most of the girls on the basketball team were also on the volleyball team. He convinced me that the fundamentals I would learn in volleyball would also increase my basketball ability, so I was sold! I did have one condition: I didn't have to wear those spandex shorts that volleyball girls had to wear.

Remember, I'm still that Tomboy, so I was all in once he agreed. I started to like playing, and shockingly, I was great at it. Then tragedy finds me. Just an ordinary day at practice, the assistant coach and one of my teammates were playing around. He spiked the volleyball, and it ended up hitting me right in the eye.

At first, I was fine. I iced it and came back to practice the next day. Then a few days later, I started to notice that I was seeing floaters. From floaters to flashing lights, which turned into rainbows.

Several days later, while I was in the gym working out, the sight in my eye completely blacked out. I called my mom, and she rushed me to the doctor, where I found out that my retina was utterly detached due to being hit by that volleyball.

This was another surgery, but the results were a little different from the previous ones. Unfortunately, this one wasn't successful. According to the doctor, he did all that he could do. But unfortunately, being hit by the ball caused too much trauma, and it was nothing he could do to save the sight in my right eye. I was devastated.

So here I am, confused as to why something like this was happening to me but too afraid to ask God why. Yet, I still couldn't focus on the negatives because I had a tough decision to make. My parents sat me down and explained my options. I could choose to stop playing ball, and they promised that they wouldn't be any less proud of me, or I could choose to keep playing, but playing with one eye wouldn't be easy. I'm sure you can guess what my decision was. I wanted to play, so my dad and I went to work.

He started training me on maneuvering on the court with one eye. It was non-stop. Even while we were at home, he would do things like roll oranges at me from different directions to train my left eye to be dominant and focus on the ball at all times.

I think I was a better player with just one eye than

with two. My sophomore year, I was joined on the court by my little sister Jawanda, who was also a top prospect. At the time, I was about six foot five, and my sister was about six foot two, and together we ran circles around those girls. They nicknamed us the Twin Towers, and colleges started offering us two-for-one package deals to come to their school.

A few of my accomplishments throughout high school were Nike All-American, Adidas All-American, McDonald's All-American, and USA All-American. By the time I was a senior in high school, I was the number two female basketball player in the nation.

The fact that I accomplished all that with sight in one eye still amazes me. I'm told I inspire others. I signed to Georgia Tech on a full scholarship.

Still, my path led me to Middle Tennessee State University instead. I absolutely hated every second of it. Although I went to MTSU on a full-ride scholarship to play ball, I never got the chance to play. Then, one day while playing a pickup game with the girls, I felt a sharp pain in my chest that caused me to drop to my knees. To this day, that pain is indescribable! I was immediately taken to the hospital where I was told the worse news of my life; my basketball career was over. I was diagnosed with a heart condition called Marfan Syndrome. It was an inherited disorder characterized particularly by skeletal changes, displacement of the eye's lens, and a tendency to develop aneurysms, especially of the aorta.

I didn't want to believe it, so I went to get several different opinions. They all told me the same thing, I had Marfan, and after researching this condition, it explained why I went through everything I went through in my younger years.

Basketball was the one thing in my life that I thought would always be there, and now it was gone. I couldn't even look at a basketball without crying. I started to hate myself. I had one mission, and I failed.

In my thought process, basketball was supposed to feed my family. I worked so hard, trained so hard, overcame every obstacle that got in my way, and still, I failed. I felt like I let my parents down, my teammates, my supporters, and most of all I let myself down.

The worst part about it was that once the coaches got the news, those folks started treating me like pure sh**. It wasn't my fault, but they treated me like it was. Once they realized I was no use to them, they treated me like a random bum on the street. I didn't deserve that. I was just a kid. Looking back, I should've just packed my things and left. Still, I knew that my parents couldn't afford to put me through college. However, my education was crucial to me, so I stayed.

Fast forward to my senior year of college. I noticed that the vision in my left eye started decreasing. Because of what happened to my right eye, I immediately took action.

My dad came to pick me up and took me to a doctor back home. The doctor looked at my eye and told me that I was experiencing some scar tissue. However, he assured me that a simple surgery would not only fix it, but it would also have me seeing out of that eye better than I ever had before. *Finally,* I thought, *some good news.* We scheduled the surgery, which ironically was on my birthday. A gift would be the recovery time for the procedure having me back in just enough time to finish out my last semester of college.

So I went into surgery, and to this day, I still don't know exactly what went wrong. I knew that something had gone wrong because when I came out of surgery, I was completely blind. After losing my sight, I went through every emotion possible—sadness, anger, depression, fear, shame, and above all, hopelessness.

I went through denial. I refused to use my cane for a long time. I tried to hide because I just couldn't wrap my mind around the fact that I went from being one of the top female basketball players in the nation to being blind.

Let me paint a picture for you all. Before I went through this, I was a pretty popular person. I ran with the big names on the girls' basketball team. I was a part of the in-crowd. I say that to say I had a lot of friends, not to mention the ones back home.

As I went through that situation, all I could wonder was, "What in the hell could I have done in my past that was so bad that God would allow something this terrible to happen to me? Because I mean bad things like this don't happen to good people, right?" Anyway, where was I?

Oh yeah, I'm going through this trying to stay strong, and then I broke. I mean, y'all, it broke me in an unexplainable way. It was then that I had reached the lowest point in my life, or so I thought.

In the midst of this, every single person in my life that called themselves a friend disappeared. Y'all, I mean every single one of them. Those friends that I would ride for and give my last to in several situations. I lost sleep over these people. I couldn't understand for the life of me why someone that called themselves my friend would walk out on me the one time I needed them.

I mean, they walked out as if that was the only option, and that shit hurt. I don't know if it bothered me more that I was the person that everybody came to when they were at low points, and I always showed up. Or if it bothered me more because I was the type of friend who never asked for much. All I needed was, "You got this, J." "Hold your head up, J." Hell, tell me a joke because, at that moment, anything was better than nothing.

However, the silver lining was I did have my family. Denise was my right hand and my best friend. The Jacksons were my second family, home away from home. Their support overshadowed the support that was missing.

Around that same time, my brother got sick. He also has Marfan Syndrome. One night while he was at work, he had a sharp pain in his chest. Because I had done so much research on Marfan Syndrome, I instantly knew what was happening. My brother was experiencing an aortic dissection, which is one of the symptoms that Marfan patients have to worry about. He was rushed to the hospital, where a doctor named William Morris Brown performed surgery that saved my brother's life.

Soon after that, my mother got extremely ill. She was in the hospital, and according to the doctors, she was dying. I'm sitting at the hospital, keeping my mother company. Well, more like talking her head off about God knows what. I broke down crying at that moment. Through those tears, I remember saying, "Ma, you gotta make it through this. Please don't leave me like everybody else."

In her weakest moments, my mother gave me some advice that completely changed my way of thinking. She used her hand to put it under my chin so that she could lift my head.

She said, "You were a good friend to all them mother******. I don't know what their reason for leaving but let them go. Focus on the people that are here and for the ones that are not *** 'em."

Now I don't know what happened in that hospital that day, but it was like God gave my mother a second chance in life. She did a one-eighty. It was like she was never sick. So in my heart, things are looking up in this part of my life.

In April of 2015, my father went into the hospital because he was experiencing swelling in his feet and legs. The medical staff ran several tests on him. Finally, they got the swelling down and were scheduled to release him to go home the next day. Not sure why but the doctors decided to run one more test on him before he was released. To our understanding, it was a routine procedure that was done often.

While my dad was in that procedure, literally everything that was supposed to go right went wrong. It resulted in my father coding and dying right in front of me. It was as if my world went utterly silent with only the sound of my grief screaming to the heavens. I'm sure you would like to think that it doesn't get any worse, right? Wrong.

Precisely four months and three days from the day my dad passed, I got a phone call from my little sister asking me if I was by myself. I could tell something was wrong from the tone in her voice. Luckily, Denise happened to be with me, so I responded I wasn't alone. She told me to come quickly because momma wouldn't wake up. I pulled up to my parent's house. My aunt Maxine walked up and hugged me before I could even make it to the door.

Now my Auntie Maxine is my safe place. She's someone that's always been there. She did so much for my siblings and me. Throughout the years, the bond we developed was unbreakable, so I trusted her like I trusted my parents.

As my aunt embraced me, she broke the news in the easiest way she knew how. I'll never forget the words she whispered to me, "Baby, she didn't make it." At that moment, I knew that it was nothing my aunt could do to fix what had happened. I reverted back to a kid for that split second as I folded in my auntie's arms and cried like a baby. I knew she was the only person I trusted to hold me up at that very moment.

Now, wait God. Let me get this straight. I lost basketball, sight, friends, my father tragically, and now I lost my mother. You're telling me I can't come to you and question these things? I could go to my dad and ask him anything. If the word is telling me that you, God, are my father, why can't I come to you with questions?

On that day, my relationship with God became my own! My spirit began to stir, and an outpour of answers began to flood my soul. I realized that not only could I question God, but He had the answers all along. He was just waiting for me to ask. That's when I heard His voice, "Demand of me because I will demand of you." And the most profound thing happened on this day. I began to heal.

I realize now that I got so wrapped up in what I wanted to do and be in life that I completely dismissed what it was that God wanted me to do, so he had to shake up a few things to get my attention. God blessed me with a gift that would allow me to heal myself and travel the world using my voice to help heal other people. That gift is spoken word. Never in a million years did I imagine that I could be someone that would touch as many lives as I have.

I'll leave you with this for now. There are some things in life that you don't want to happen but have to accept. Some things will be tempting to the eye, yet you still must reject. Some things you will be forced to learn, yet really don't want to know, and some people you feel you can't live without you have to let go.

Lynette Eberhardt

It Ain't Over

"Why should I feel discouraged,
Why should the shadows come?
Why should my heart feel lonely,
And long for Heaven and home?
When Jesus is my portion,
A constant friend is He.
His eye is on the sparrow
And I know He watches over me.
Why should I feel discouraged—"

"What is she singing?" one of the technicians asked.

"Why should the shadows come?" I continued worshiping.

"His Eye Is on the Sparrow." The surgeon replied.

"Why should my heart feel lonely."

"I don't know it." The technician was still lost.

"And long for Heaven and home."

"Really? Really? Are you really interrupting me right now while I'm trying to sing? I'm trying to praise my way through this and you—"

I noticed the surgeon give the anesthesiologist a look as the O.R. grew quiet during my tirade. Then, obeying the surgeon's non-verbal queue, he attached the syringe and pressed the plunger. He told me that he was administering medicine to help calm me. The other technicians continued to prep and strap me to the surgical table.

Tears stung my eyes. "My life is over!" Those were the last words spoken before I went under the anesthesia. It was 2011. I was having surgery to kill the nerve endings in my right eye because the magnitude of pain was so great. I'm talking so bad (worse than a migraine) that my fiancée had to invest in blackout curtains and WD-40 for the door hinge.

I lost almost 40 pounds from not eating, and I tried negotiating with God to kill me. In return, I would never ask Him for anything in life again. Glaucoma is nothing to play with. Add to that retinal detachment, and you have a recipe for disaster.

During this process, other health issues appeared. In walks a diagnosis of end-stage renal failure on top of diabetes and neuropathy in my hands and feet... baby, listen.

Wait. First, allow me to introduce myself. My name is Lynette Eberhardt. However, I go by Lyn with one N, milk chocolate skin, and intriguing eyes—one the color of rich earth, the other of cloudy skies. I'm telling you now, I'm a little wild, over the top, and sometimes too expressive, but stay with me. I promise there is a moral to this story.

Now pause. Let's rewind. I always had vision issues. In the third grade, my teacher Ms. D noticed me squinting at the blackboard in math. She knew that I excelled in that subject, so she reached out to my parents when I started failing pop quizzes written on the board.

Of course, they took immediate action and scheduled an appointment. The issue was that money was tight due to my mother getting laid off and going from a two-income household down to one.

I had to get affordable glasses and, honey, let me tell you, I was not trying to wear those humongous, pink, grandma-looking glasses with the arms that connected at the bottom of the frame! Time progressed, and eventually, I just stopped wearing glasses. My parents stopped wasting money buying them.

Fast forward to 2000. I was living on my own and paid off the first vehicle that I purchased myself and had a nice paying job at that time. I decided I wanted to ride in style. I started leasing a brand-new Ford Explorer 2-door Sport, black with grey trim, power everything, and a moon roof—precisely what I wanted!

A few months in, I noticed that I couldn't read the numbers on the radio buttons. What the heck? I went to the doctor and received a diagnosis that I had cataracts in both eyes. My original lenses had to be removed, and cataracts were lasered and vacuumed out to correct the problem.

After, an acrylic lens was placed back in my eyes. This was done one eye at a time and approximately six weeks between. Let me tell you. After that first procedure, when I looked out the window and noticed the veins of the leaves for the first time ever in my life, I cried with gratitude and amazement.

Let's flash forward some more to approximately 2010. I previously attained an associate degree in accounting technology (2005) and business management (2009). Deciding to further my education and obtain a bachelor's in business administration, I started a two-year program. Nine months in, I noticed that I was having difficulty driving home at night, so I switched to day classes. Around month eleven, there was difficulty reading the whiteboard even though I was sitting in the front row. That's when it happened. Driving home, I stopped to get something to eat at the Pizza Hut/Taco Bell combo restaurant. Not able to read the menu board, I assumed it was due to the sun's glare. However, easing forward and around the side of the building, it became apparent that my lack of ability to read the menu was not due to the sun's brightness.

With a heavy heart, I placed my order and proceeded home. That fifteen-minute drive seemed to last forty minutes. I couldn't see the taillights of the vehicles ahead of me until I was almost on their bumpers; this happened at three of the four lights before reaching my house. Realizing that I didn't trust my judgment to cross through the last light, I pulled into the nearest parking lot, bawled like a baby, and called my fiancée to come to get me. Those last three minutes home were pure torture following close behind, knowing I may be parking my car indefinitely.

We moved from Northern Kentucky to Georgia in late spring/early summer and got married in the fall of 2011. Soon after, it became apparent that I needed dialysis. Everything within me was screaming, "Don't do it!" Because I remembered being little and hearing, "You know so and so just went on dialysis. They will be gone within a year." Also, a complication from dialysis and moving ports resulted in my Mama getting an infection and sepsis and passing in 2007. That hit me very hard, and it took over a year to somewhat get myself back to some sort of normalcy.

I fought it tooth and nail until the heaviness of feeling like s*** became too unbearable. That was Spring 2013. Dialysis consisted of having two giant needles shoved into my arm in a freezing room with some weird people for four hours a day, three days a week. This also meant putting up with "know-it-all" nurses and technicians who didn't want to listen when I said that the needle wasn't in the right place and my arm could atrophy.

I imagine it's more challenging when the person you love goes through several physical and emotional changes. For example, after I had the doctor kill the nerve endings in my right eye, it caused it to turn blue, then gray. Already using a four-prong walking cane due to balance issues from the neuropathy, and now having two large humps on my left arm from dialysis didn't exactly make me look or feel attractive and really messed with my self-esteem.

In my spouse's efforts to "protect" me, I started feeling lonely and neglected when we stopped going places or spending quality time together. It got to the point that I stopped going to my in-laws' house on holidays and just stayed home either by myself or with the dogs. Divorce was spoken often, and the realization of a failed marriage was on the horizon. Now let me be clear… I don't want to paint a picture that my spouse just turned away because of my circumstances. Marriage is hard work. My grief at times was heavy, and in the process, I lashed out. Other times, I either pushed away or was needy. It was a perfect storm with the changes within me and other personal issues in my spouse's life. As a result, we couldn't be or give the full support the other needed.

During one of these moments of solitude, I found myself down in the dumps, hell, below the dumps! I indulged in a prodigious pity party in total isolation and complete silence. After my "woe is me" moment, I lay in the middle of the bed in the fetal position bawling my eyes out. Then, remembering what the elders and preachers used to say, I began praising and worshipping the Most-High God through my pain and tears.

Throwing all formalities away, I bared my soul and had a conversation with Him. Sayings such as, "God is bigger than your anger at Him," and "He'll never put more on you than you can bear," raced through my thoughts.

"God! Oh, God! I can't continue to do this! You say that You won't put more on me than I can bear. I guess You see more in me than I do, but this is too much for me! I want to give up on life, but you know that I'm too much of a coward to off myself. Do you hate me? I know that I need to do better in my walk; I know I'm guilty of not giving You my all… this is too damn much! My Mama is gone; my dad doesn't f*** with me. Okay, sorry for cursing. Sorry. My marriage is failing—yeah, I know it wasn't in Your plan. What the f***? Sorry. I did it again… I'm just so frustrated! Something's gotta give! Please, God, please! Either bring back my eyesight in my one eye (both eyes would be a greater testimony) or let me get my transplant. Please let me get a donor with a matching kidney and pancreas; both would be great, but one or the other… Puh-lease!"

Crying to the point of no more tears and dry heaving, a sense of calm overtook me. It was so surreal. Unsure if I was asleep or in some sort of trance, I noticed my surroundings turning a shade of deep maroon or burgundy.

I felt as though I was floating and ascending. So

many sheer, white veils moved out of my way as I continued ascending. A bright, white light or energy beyond made me tremble. I became petrified and unworthy of getting any closer. I know this may sound a little outlandish. Still, an unspoken communication told me to stay steadfast with some chastisement. My feeling of uneasiness and unworthiness overtook me.

Questioning if this experience was real or a trick of 'the enemy' caused me to lose the "connection" and descend. Coming out of whatever state of being I was in, I still felt some peace. I began to listen to different church services online and began working on bettering myself. I started speaking life over myself and speaking healing and continued praying that one if not both of these major setbacks in my life would be rectified.

Within several months, I received a call for a potential transplant. The excitement in the house amongst family and friends was palpable. Unfortunately, I was a backup plan to several others on the list if they weren't a match.

Going home defeated that my prayer wasn't answered, I took a few days to regroup and give God the praise for blessing someone else because someday that would be me. These calls came once a year, starting in 2013.

"The third time's the charm!" That is what I told family, friends, and the physicians while on the floor for final testing and prep, smiling from ear to ear.

After my nephrologist explained how he didn't like how the organs looked, I went home distraught. He also didn't feel comfortable transplanting since they came from a former inmate with several 'jailhouse' tattoos; they were susceptible to hepatitis.

In 2017, I turned forty and decided to finally knock Hawaii off my bucket list. But unfortunately, being on dialysis brewed a massive hindrance to my vacation. My treatment was in the middle of the day and prevented several activities and excursions.

So while I watched a beautiful sunset amongst the palm trees over the vastness of the Pacific Ocean as the sky turned shades of yellow, pink, and orange, I prayed again. God, please. Something has to give.

Months later, I was introduced to The National Federation of the Blind (NFB). The President of the newly formed chapter suggested I attend a leadership meeting in February 2018. I met a few positive people who have been very influential in my growth in accepting my blindness/visual impairment. I also connected with influential blind/low-vision individuals.

Two weeks later, I received a call from the transplant coordinator. The call was rather odd. She started the call by asking about other health issues pertaining to foot ulcers, mammograms, and perceived heart concerns.

I told her all these matters had been resolved

over a year prior. The information should have been updated in the system, so there shouldn't be any reason I was ineligible on the transplant list.

Her mode of questioning remained terse and odd, out of the ordinary, until finally, I asked, "Wait! Is this your way of telling me y'all found a match?"

She confirmed a strong possibility and scheduled me for an after-hours mammogram. Once tested, I gave approximately nine vials of blood. They made sure a scratch from my dog was only a surface wound and uninfected. After that, I was given the green light to go home and wait for further instruction.

"Thank You, God! Thank You! Thank You! Thank You! I'm praising and thanking You in advance for all You've done and are about to do. I believe that what You have for me is for me, and it is for me this time! I doubt because we've been down this road four times before… then, where is my faith, right? I have to trust You… No, I'm going to trust You… No, I do trust You! This is it! Thank You!"

I've had my share of ups and downs, times when there was no one around, God came and spoke these words to me, Praise will confuse the enemy… I started singing, I started clapping, I started dancing, people were laughing, they knew my problems, they knew my pain, but I knew God would take 'em away…

My phone rang, interrupting my praise and worship session with "Praise Him in Advance" by Marvin Sapp. Seeing it was the transplant coordinator,

I took a deep breath, fearing the worst yet hoping for the best. She simply asked how soon I could make it to the hospital. I screamed and told her two hours after apologizing for practically blowing her eardrum out.

Immediately, I ate two healthy plates of spaghetti because I knew there was no eating or drinking after midnight. Then, I showered in anti-bacterial soap and surgical hospital soap. I packed a small duffle bag with my phone, charger, iPad, and blanket. I put on some comfy pajamas and headed to the hospital.

It was explained that the organs were coming from Atlanta to Augusta. The unfortunate donor family was in the process of saying their last goodbyes before pulling the plug. One of the technicians told me the donor was a young male in a dreadful motorcycle accident. Mixed emotions overtook me as I weighed the family's hurt, grieving their loss and my impending happiness.

We reached out to family and friends via phone and social media as time progressed. We petitioned for prayers that the organs would be a match with no hiccups this time. Finally, sometime in the wee hours of the morning, two surgeons came to the room, briefing me on the procedure to transplant the kidney and the pancreas.

"So, does this mean everything is a go?" I asked them.

The surgeons confirmed and stated the organs were almost in route. I was scheduled to have my last dialysis treatment to ensure that my blood was clean and that my body was ready to receive this gift.

"Hallelujah!" I belted out.

Some of the nurses and technicians looked in the room disapprovingly of my loud outburst, but I didn't care. I thanked my God! My family prayed and shared the excellent news, asking for more prayers that everything would be successful.

Unfortunately, many complications occurred during the surgery. The procedures lasted three hours longer than anticipated. I was drugged heavily and didn't remember my spouse and family seeing me post-op.

However, I remember a team coming into the ICU room and telling me that I had to be rushed back into surgery. The pancreas wasn't working correctly, and they feared a blood clot. I was able to shake the haze of the medicine and demand they call my spouse to inform of the imminent emergency surgery.

What should have only been a few weeks in the hospital turned into a month. I had sepsis, and there were more problems with clotting in the pancreas. Once I was finally released home in mid-March, I found myself thankful and thoughtful about my blessing.

The morning of my one-week follow-up, I woke up several hours early to wash up and get ready for the appointment. I moved rather slowly. Not to be too graphic, I went to use the bathroom somewhat in the dark and heard water spilling on the floor. When I went to wash my hands, I checked the his and her sinks, the garden tub, and I knew it wasn't the stand-alone shower. *Hmmm, what in the world?*

Well, let me just say my kidney was working fine. I had to relieve myself before setting my shower chair to wash up in front of the sink. Then, I heard the water sound again. Now, I know I'm not going crazy... I flipped the light on and noticed a puddle of blood on the rug and a trail everywhere I walked to check the potential water source. My freaking stomach had sprung a leak where the surgeons had made their long incision.

Alerting my spouse, we called 911 and the transplant clinic, informing them of what was occurring. Once again, I had to spend several weeks in the hospital. Apparently, I developed a large hematoma (a pool of blood).

The surgeons had to drain and scrape the dead tissue where the blood was sitting. Without being overly descriptive, I'll just describe my open stomach area as the shape of the head and base of a snowman. It looked like raw hamburger meat. The doctors sent me home with a wound vac.

Many more complications occurred, including a stomach ulcer, a severe reaction to Fentanyl patches, and other meds causing me to hallucinate, sleep all day, become very combative, and my blood pressure dropping to dangerously low numbers. I was in and out of the hospital from February 21st to November 4th. I think I was home a total of eight weeks, hit or miss. A week here, a few days there, and I managed to stay out the whole month of September. At one point, I wondered if the transplant was truly worth the trouble.

During one of my extended stays, my BP dropped to 57/43. I thought for sure that I would check out and meet my maker. I couldn't understand why the nurses and doctors weren't shooting me up with saline solutions as they had done before?

I was wearing a necklace with a tiny mustard seed. I clenched it tightly and reminded myself to have faith! I was so scared that I couldn't even pray properly. All I could say was, "Oh, God! Oh, God! Help me! Please forgive me of any sins known and unknown to me! I'm not ready to die! Why would You have me go through all of this just to let me die? Oh, God! Oh, God! Oh, God."

Seemingly after forever, the nurse finally administered a few pints of blood for a transfusion. This happened a total of eight times. My faith grew stronger through my healing processes (yes, plural), and I could think over my life. I vowed to commit to doing better in my walk with the Lord and figuratively grab life by the horns and ride the heck out of it!

I met someone that showed me that I could still be me even though I am visually impaired. I started gaining some of my independence back and going places without the help or guidance of my spouse. I started traveling and restoring some confidence.

I met some more positive, independent, goal-oriented, and working blind people and decided to surround myself with those types of individuals for motivation and support.

Although I'm not where I want to be in life, I am further than I was after initially losing sight. I currently co-chair a peer support group called Looking Forward and have been asked to co-chair another peer support group and a women's ministry. I am a member of the Community Service Division of the NFB and enjoy partaking in activities that reach out to other blind/low-vision individuals and giving back to the community. I also do small tasks like prepping bags with needed items such as Bibles, toothbrushes, toothpaste, deodorant, socks, masks, hand sanitizer, bottled water, etc., for distribution to the homeless with my religious organization.

Currently, I am learning JAWS (Job Access with Speech) which is basically a talking computer, and about to start mobility training since things are getting dimmer daily. My dream is to finish out my bachelor's degree.

However, I'm unsure if I want to stick to the accounting field or pursue a different avenue. Advocating for the rights of the blind and other disabilities is something that I enjoy. I like to call myself a liaison because I'm good at putting people in touch with other productive blind people who can help or give the necessary resources. They can obtain the needed information or skills to achieve their goals and endeavors. I guess the moral of my story is to always keep the faith. I believe in the Most- High God. Surround yourself with a positive, supportive circle, and it's never too late to get your life in order. I've been visually impaired for approximately ten years, and I am just learning who the new Lyn with one N is, but honey, let me tell you… I am a force to be reckoned with. Unless The Creator chooses to call me home, you will know my name! That's in the blind community and hopefully beyond. My old life is over. This new one has just begun! Prayerfully, you'll be hearing from me soon.

Samuel Jonita Gates

A Blind One's Vision

What kind of pain was this that stopped me in my tracks? Then brought me to my knees as I covered my eyes with my hands. Tears seeped between my fingers and rolled down my hands from the pressure and sensation of ripping behind my eyeballs. "Oh, God!" I screamed. It had been just a minute ago that I was casually walking toward the kitchen to find my favorite thing—food. Now, what was happening to me? I stumbled then wobbled to the sofa, praying and hoping after I lay down, the pain would go away as I relaxed and rested. Unfortunately, relaxation did not come. The pain did not go away.

Instead, I felt a more intense tightening and feeling of pulling or ripping apart, seemingly behind and all through my eyeballs. I lay there, trying to press on my eyelids without causing more pain, just for a bit of relief. Seconds then minutes passed, I slightly stroked across my eyelids then up and down my forehead, but nothing seemed to alleviate the pain. Excruciating would have initially described this, but now there are new words to describe this pain—agonizing and tormenting. Not only do I feel this physically, but it now extends to my mind as my head began to ache due to confused thoughts of what could be wrong.

I didn't have any forewarnings or symptoms that could have alerted me to investigate or prepare for anything like this. It was just *bam,* and it was happening. I had experienced the pain of this magnitude one other time in my life. I have been known to have a high pain tolerance. That's to say, I endured the pain throughout most of my life without complaining, without taking medications, or without visiting a doctor or hospital. This experience changed many things in my life.

Returning to the association or mental connection of the one other time that such an experience with pain invaded my physical body would be in childbirth. My firstborn was what anyone would call an easy labor and delivery. I didn't have any pain during labor while I waited to dilate enough to give birth. I read comic books and worked crossword puzzles until they told me it was time. In and out, they had come to check me, did so, then went back and continued to wait. The only discomfort came with the pushing. I thought, "*Would I ever be able to push hard enough to bring this baby forth from my womb?*"

Of course, I did, but I questioned it. It was not easy or painless with my second and third children. Since I was young, I felt that I didn't know all I should have known about marriage, conceiving, and giving birth. I thought with each forthcoming pregnancy that it would be another easy labor and delivery. Even after the painful labor with my second, I still expected the third to be like the first. I fasted and prayed consistently with the first child for an easy, painless labor and delivery, which seemed to have made a tremendous difference. I didn't do the same with these two because I felt unworthy to ask God for such a thing again. But that's another story.

Again, as with the first, each time after that, my water broke. Even though my water broke, neither of these children wanted to come from the comfort of my womb and enter this world to see their awaiting mother. With the premature rupture of membranes, amniotic fluid depleted before I dilated enough to deliver. The doctor was concerned about infection with leaking amniotic fluid and still no labor. So induced labor medication was administered...then came the pain!

The pain that caused me to pray. "Oh, God, if you cannot take this pain away for some reason, take me out of this world to be home with You." I felt and believed I could not bear this and live through it.

That's enough about that association of the pain. It was challenging to omit from this writing because both experiences with pain were similar, and my reactions were the same—God deliver me or take me home. Now here I am again with a pain of the same magnitude and depth, causing me to cry out to God. I kept believing it would be gone sooner or later.

Preferably sooner, not later. Sooner it was not. I wanted to grab my eyeballs and yank them from the sockets.

I pleaded with Jesus to intercede for me to the Father and deliver His child from this pain. Then as abruptly as it had come, it was gone. When the pain ceased, I remained on the sofa. I considered going to the doctor since I was mobile again and functional enough to drive. Still, my hatred of doctor and hospital visits convinced me that it was over, and everything was okay.

As time passed, my vision began to be extremely blurred and cloudy. I noticed little black spots, yellow squiggly lines, and floaters in my sight. Thinking that I had gone too long without wearing my eyeglasses, I decided to see the Optometrist because the glasses were broken. He informed me of what he observed and that any glasses would not help, and neither could he. He suggested that I see an Ophthalmologist immediately. I asked what would happen if I did not see this doctor. He said that I would probably lose my ability to see and eventually become blind.

I went home thinking of the only words or takeaway I got from this visit—*be blind.*

My thoughts were racing from one to another as if they were competing to be the first-place winner for inducing fear and a state of despondency within me. It would all be due to thinking of things that would change if I became sightless. It is funny how people prioritize things and the reasons they do.

The first thing at the top of the list dealt with family. I considered my unhappiness if I wouldn't be able to see my granddaughter that my daughter would birth nor my grandson that my second son would father. It seems that the thought of not seeing my forthcoming grandchildren was placed first before I concerned myself with the work of the ministry for God. That is surprising to me since I usually think spiritual before natural.

Nonetheless, while waiting for time to pass for my scheduled appointment day to arrive, I considered blindness and how it would bring about many changes in how I live. The unexpected is the unexpected. Yes, it is. I would never have given thought to blindness being an issue in my lifetime, not even in my old age. But here I am, thinking of the possible lifestyle change due to being blind. First, there would be the inability to read and research scripture independently. I would become the passenger, not the driver. I would not have the sight to bring all the things in my creative mind to fruition. I would go from independent to dependant, which would be my way of life. I would be forced to embrace the inability to take care of my needs and not see the beauty in the world anymore. Not to mention my inability to see approaching danger.

All the listed concerns were major to me, but the minor things also made a significant difference. I would not be able to match my clothing, jewelry, shoes, stockings, or socks just to step out in a mixed-matched ensemble. I couldn't see my hairstyle. I wouldn't know what I was putting in my mouth to eat. I would be confined and imprisoned within the four walls of my dwelling place with many more thoughts. I was convinced that not being able to see meant my life would be over, and death would be far better than being blind, a pathetic existence of dependency.

This thought remained with me more after the Ophthalmologist informed me that I would not regain any of the vision that I had lost and would continue to lose sight until I was completely blind. I needed to have surgery to reattach my detached retinas. I also had to control my diabetes and high blood pressure. The detaching of my retinas was what was happening to me that day of excruciating pain. The condition is known as Diabetic Retinopathy. It becomes severe with uncontrolled glucose levels and high blood pressure, leading to detachment of the retinas and blindness. Now, how will I live fully, confidently, independently, autonomously, productively, effectively, ambitiously, prospering, and so on?

Trying to see became challenging in small ways as I pondered whether to undergo surgery or not. Therefore, I began to do as much as I could and prepared for the possibility of total blindness just in case it came quicker than predicted. During the waiting period, my ability to see clearly was diminishing. Some things became difficult to do, and the lack of dependable transportation sparked anger and frustration.

The anger of my situation and the frustration of my inabilities was becoming an every-other-day thing. Thoughts of ceasing it all remained on my mind. One day as I sat beneath the tall pine trees of East Texas, I cried. I remember looking up and around at all the beauty I would not see if I were totally blind. Thinking and considering was not going to change the situation nor change the doctor's words that the surgery was not guaranteed to fix the problem. It's possible it would cause more vision loss.

Thinking did cause me to remember the source that gave me the breath of life and sustained it every day with whatever was needed. So I prayed! I begin to talk to God and express my thoughts, fears, and desires. I told Him that I didn't want to live without being able to see nor be able to take care of myself and not have to depend on others. After pouring out my heart, I praised Him, thanked Him, and then sat quietly, focusing only on Him and waiting for any sign or word from Him. Then scriptures and words came quickly into my head, and I heard the answer to my dilemma. Do I continue to live with legal or total blindness, or do I seek death? The first words heard in my head were, "Why are you fearful or saddened? God is still God, the Great I Am, the Sustainer." I felt ashamed when hearing the things spoken in my head and called to my attention, primarily what I already knew, should have remembered, known to believe, and stand on faithfully.

First and foremost, *I belong to God. I am not my own*. I can't decide just to exist or to end my life. God gave me life and His timing for the end of that life. He had already looked down the path of my life before I was born and decided how every mistake or success in my life could be used for His purpose and glory. Therefore, I needed to surrender to His will to fulfill His preordained will and purpose for my life.

Knowing God had a plan for me and work to complete for Him gave me the motivation, desire, and will, even blind, to "live deliberately," as the phrase coined by Henry David Thoreau states and as Tim McGraw's song title states, "*Live Like You Were Dying*." So be it. I will live deliberately and do all I can every day as if I were dying.

In addition, He revealed to me that I would still be able to sing messages that teach and admonish (warn, encourage, advise). I would still be able to hear or have the scriptures read to me so that I could pray for understanding from the Holy Spirit then share the Word. I could continue collecting for the needy, telephone and visit the homebound, write my books, poems, plays, songs, or whatever.

There are too many strategies and ways to take care of myself. I acknowledged that the God-given vision of my future was so clear and detailed that a blind person could fulfill it or bring it to fruition. That would be me. “It is not about the sight lost, but the vision gained,” as this book’s subtitle states. Amen.

Stacie Leap

Take a Leap of Faith

My name is Stacie. I have been blind since January 2016 because of a domestic violence relationship. The boyfriend I had at the time attacked me repeatedly. Through the constant abuse, I ended up with three dislocated vertebral discs in the cervical section of my spine, ongoing lower back pain, and vision loss in both of my eyes.

The vertebral discs in my neck were dislocated in December 2015. I had to wear a C-spine collar four months before surgery because I was also two months pregnant. The doctors wanted to perform neck surgery to replace the vertebral discs with bone, which required anesthesia. Still, I had to wait until my second trimester because I was very early in my pregnancy. The doctors told me that the anesthesia would be very harmful to the unborn child so early in the pregnancy. I had to wear the C-spine collar 24/7, even in the shower, because if I moved my neck the wrong way or moved sharply, I could risk harming my spinal cord, resulting in death.

In January 2016, after repeated punches and

blows to my face, I saw a sudden flash of light, thinking that my vision would come back because when he hit me before, my vision would blur but then come back in a matter of hours. However, this time was not the case. My vision became blurry, and eventually, I could not see anything at all. During one of my prenatal appointments, I told the doctors that I could not sign any paperwork because I could not see. I was immediately admitted to the hospital.

The doctors examined me and told me that my retinas were detached in both of my eyes. They asked me what happened, but I was scared to tell them because my ex-boyfriend had come with me to the hospital. I kept telling them that I did not know what happened. I did not want him angry at me and hurt me when I went back home because we lived together. Also, I did not want to risk losing my baby.

After a week in the hospital, the doctors told me that I could leave and return home. However, I was living at my ex-boyfriend's house at the time, so I was petrified to go back. I ended up telling the social worker at the hospital that I had no place to go and that I wanted to get away from him. I thought about the consequences if I ended up going back to him. I was pregnant and did not want my child to be born in that environment. Also, because of my new blindness, I felt that he would not assist me and possibly die from another beating.

When he realized that I would not return, he told

me that I could not get any of my stuff back. He said he would sell everything and throw away the things he could not. I was despondent and devastated that I had no belongings. The only things I owned were the clothes I went to the hospital in. At the same time, I was relieved that I escaped him. But, on the other hand, I was terrified that I was all alone with no belongings, no eyesight, no home, and no money while carrying a baby. I was so depressed during my entire pregnancy because I thought I was worth so little. I blamed myself for everything.

The social worker at the hospital was able to refer me to an outside behavioral health agency. They assigned a case manager who helped me get things in place once discharged. She also listened to all my anxieties, fears, and worries. She looked into getting a therapist to work through my emotions and trauma. The case manager and social worker worked together alongside the doctors and staff members of both agencies to connect me with many resources to help me.

I ended up staying at the hospital recuperating from my injuries until my surgeries in May for my neck and eyes. The neck surgery went well. I could move my neck again and not risk injuring my spine if I moved too sharply. Unfortunately, my eyesight never returned even after two surgeries.

Throughout the entire hospital stay, my ex-boyfriend continued to visit me at the hospital. I had to restrict visitation and file for a Protection from Abuse order. I could not go to family court to file for a PFA since I was still admitted to the hospital. I had to do it over the phone. His mother helped get me the PFA. She came to visit me at the hospital, and I told her what happened. She traveled to the courts on my behalf to pick up the documents for me to sign and then helped me bring the documents to his local police station to serve him the PFA.

After my surgeries, I was transferred to a physical rehabilitation facility. I had occupational therapy where the occupational therapist helped me modify ways to live independently. For example, I label my clothing and supplies. My clothing was tagged with safety pins in various patterns. Those different patterns meant the other colors. My bottles were marked with tape or rubber bands to differentiate them (shampoo, conditioner, lotion, body wash, etc.).

I was also taught how to identify currency coins by their size and feel. I was also taught some Braille by the recreational therapist there. I also had a physical therapist who helped me learn how to move up and down steps safely and walk around outside with a sighted guide. They helped me get a free white cane from the NFB. Once I received that, they showed me how to use it. They also helped connect me with PA's Bureau of the Blind and Visually Impaired to get more formal and proper training.

During my stay at the rehab, I was still very

depressed and expressed my worries to the staff there. Being a parent, I was concerned for my safety and wanted to learn ways to manage my life. I was so thankful that the therapists at the rehab listened to me. They tried their best to see what they could do to help me adapt and modify things for my future home, wherever that would be. The nurses at the nurses' station helped gather clothes and toiletries for me. They bought me clothes for my baby. During their downtime or breaks, they would come into my room and sit to listen to me cry or pray over me.

They told me stories of what they did when their kids were little. I listened very hard and tried to memorize everything they told me. I was determined to be a better mother. I told myself that I needed to learn everything I could to be ready for my baby. I made sure I attended every session and activity at that rehab. I was still dealing with the emotion of my trauma and loss of sight, but I was trying to make the most of the situation and learn to be better.

I spent a month at the rehab until my case manager found me temporary housing until she could locate something more permanent. I was placed with a woman at her house temporarily. She offered me a room and helped me with meals. During my time there, I was given some home care services. For example, a home health aide came for an hour to assist with hygiene, grooming, and organizing my items.

An occupational therapist marked different areas

around the house to assist me with getting to them easier and identifying them. A physical therapist helped me learn to use the white cane to navigate the stairs and around the house. I received an evaluation from the Bureau of Blindness and Visual Services and was told that I would start receiving services in a few weeks. I was also connected with a doula who came weekly to listen to me and help me learn some ways to take care of myself and take care of a baby once my baby is born.

I was elated that I was slowly receiving services for myself and learning ways to do things for my baby, such as changing diapers, breastfeeding techniques, swaddling, and other tips and tricks. I felt a little better that I had all these supports to assist me when I didn't know what to do.

My caseworker found me a one-bedroom apartment at the end of May. I was expected to move at the beginning of June. That way, I could learn how to navigate my new apartment before the baby arrived. My case manager helped me find furniture and supplies for the apartment. I was very excited to be on my own again and happy that these services were coming into place. I wanted to make sure that I had a secure home for my baby when she arrived in this world.

However, during my prenatal check-up in early June, I was diagnosed with preeclampsia and was admitted back into the hospital. My blood pressure was very high, and I was placed on medication. After a few days of my blood pressure not lowering, I had to get my labor induced.

On the day that my labor was induced, I had a lot of pain. I dilated only one centimeter, and it would not get any further even with being induced. A balloon catheter was used to expand my cervix to five centimeters in hopes of starting the labor process. It worked, but it stayed that way for twenty-four hours. After a while, my baby's heartbeat dropped while mine increased.

The doctor was fearful that I might have a seizure and risk losing the baby, so they did an emergency C-section. In the end, my daughter was born at nineteen inches and five pounds, eight ounces a month early. She was automatically taken to the NICU, and I could not hold her for the first few hours of her life. I was unable to move out of my bed for two days. The doctors had to put my daughter under supervision because she had severe jaundice. In addition, they wanted to check her for trauma relating to the abuse I went through while I was pregnant with her.

While my daughter was in the NICU, I was also in ICU. So we both ended up being patients of the hospital for nineteen days. During that time, the social worker at the hospital was putting services in place for me to get home care. She also informed BBVS that I went into preterm labor and could not start my services until I recovered and was discharged.

Before being discharged from the hospital, the nurses and doctors wanted me to stay at their "Parenting Room" overnight with my daughter. They stated that they wanted to make sure I could take care of my child overnight before taking her home. Because of my anxiety about parenting, I agreed. I thought this would mean an extra day to get assistance from all the nurses until I was left to do it myself. My daughter was connected to a heart monitor, which allowed the nurses to track her progress without coming into the room.

The first day that I went home, my friend stayed the night to help me unpack my things and help me watch over my daughter when I was busy or asleep. Over the next few weeks, I was connected to a public health nurse home visiting program where a nurse would be a part of my daughter's first five years of life. The nurse taught me about baby development and ways to parent without sight. It was a learning experience for both me and the agency. I felt better because I had the support from them to make sure I could learn or sign up for various things and activities.

I was also connected to local non-profits for parents, where I attended parenting classes and learned a great deal from other parents. They helped me with my daughter's clothes, shoes, and supplies through both agencies. Both helped me emotionally and mentally as I learned about parenting and became more comfortable with my blindness.

Honestly, I was very scared all the time. I was so scared for my safety. I could not see anymore and was very fearful that my ex would find me, follow me home, and harm myself or the baby. I feared doing something wrong or someone calling to have my daughter taken from me. I was upset that I couldn't do the things I did before or enjoy things like I used to, like driving, drawing, walking around, and window shopping.

I also felt dumb and stupid for staying in a relationship for so long and not leaving before losing my eyesight. I thought it was why I couldn't see my daughter and how adorable she was like everybody told me. I was furious at everybody because I thought, "Who are they to see my daughter smile and I am her mother? I can never see her in front of my face or in my arms." I had so many feelings and emotions that couldn't be described in words. I cried every day and night as I processed everything I had to do and everything I had to learn all over again.

I finally received services from BBVS. Through them, I began getting connected to different individuals who were blind and different agencies. I learned various ways to do things around the house and care for my baby. Over the years, I attended many classes and workshops on home adaptations and parenting. I wanted to make sure I could do everything I could for my family.

When my daughter started going to head start, I

volunteered at her school in the office. I was also a part of the parent policy council. I wanted to make sure that I knew how to help in her education and get people to see that even though I have a disability, I can do everything a sighted parent can do.

I started to reach out to my networks before I went blind and tried to support the behavioral health field. I wanted to obtain my past job as a certified peer specialist and work with those in recovery and those who experienced behavioral health challenges.

Life seemed to be going in a positive direction. However, in September 2020, my ex-boyfriend came back into my life. He called me and told me that he paid to get my phone number and knows where I live. He stated that he wanted custody of my daughter and that my PFA was over. He could visit me anytime that he wants. He also told others that I was incapable of taking care of her since I couldn't see.

This made me very frantic. I spent the past four years forgetting him and moving on from the trauma I experienced from the abuse. I tried to learn ways to live with my blindness and make my life better to be a better parent for my daughter. When he called me, I felt helpless and thought that I would never escape him. I quickly called the police. They provided me with the contact information for the family court to get another PFA since the PFA that I had back in 2016 expired in 2019. In the end, I was able to get the PFA for three years which is the maximum in Pennsylvania.

At this current phase of my life, I have gained so much more knowledge and networking opportunities with other people who are blind and visually impaired. I connected with my local chapter of the National Federation of the Blind. Through all the amazing mentors and friends I have met, they pushed me to thrive for even greater. I was nominated for a board position for the Keystone chapter based in Philadelphia. I became more involved with the Pennsylvania Association of Blind Students and the National Association of Blind Students. Through all the struggles of early parenting, I was able to connect with other blind parents within the NFB. I started the PA's Blind Parents Group, where blind parents come together and share our stories, resources, and compassion. My ultimate goal is to keep breaking all the barriers in my path and show my daughter that disability is not the end but a beginning.

Daria Bannerman

Newborn Vision

I was born Saturday, May 27th, 1989, two days before Memorial Day. I weighed a whopping one pound and seven ounces. I could fit in the palm of your hand. Doctors told my family to bury me because I would not survive. Babies that small usually don't. But because my family knew the Lord and proceeded to pray for me and exercise their faith, I lived. God has a purpose for my life. There was no way I could have known this when I was born.

In fact, I wouldn't know God's purpose in my life until my early twenties. I wondered what my life would be like if I were not born prematurely. I was supposed to have been born in September. I would have been a part of the Virgo nation! Honestly, knowing that the Lord has a purpose for my life keeps me from dwelling on how different my life would have been had circumstances been different. God allowed me to live when the doctors declared I would die!

In the natural, I should have died, but in the supernatural, God was working things out for my good! I probably should have been dead. But in the supernatural, God had a plan and purpose for my life

I pray that this chapter in *The Write 2 Heal* anthology will be a blessing to you, the reader. My hope and prayer are that you gain inspiration, wisdom, and encouragement as you read these life-affirming and encouraging words.

I find my life when I lose it in you.

I gain control when I give it to you.

I save myself when I let you save me.

The best thing I can do for me is you.

– Jonathan McReynolds "Best Thing"

The summer of 2016 was interesting. I had just turned twenty-seven, and I was feeling a little adventurous. I visited various relatives, tried Sweet Frog for the first time, ate bacon and cheese sandwiches (I love bacon, obviously), and got some new clothes. I attended a family reunion at Jones' Lake and just took time to relax from a semester of grad school that seemed to drain the life out of me. One particular day, July 30th, to be exact, I was looking at a light either in the living room or the kitchen. I went to a family reunion that day and had been home from that event for about two hours. It looked dimmer than usual to me.

"Mom, is the light on?"

"Yeah, Daria," she said.

"But it looks dim to me."

"It's not dim."

I plopped down in the oversized recliner in the middle of the living room floor and tried to focus on what was on T.V. but to no avail. I kept thinking that something with my eyes was not right, but I didn't want to believe this. As a result, I got up and attempted to look at the kitchen light again.

"I can't see it that well," I told my mom. "What's happening? My eyes and head hurt."

"Well, I'll call an eye doctor and set up an appointment.

Before the appointment, I tried to calm myself down to avoid feeling anxious. "I'll Just Say Yes" by Brian Courtney Wilson was in heavy rotation. Mouthing the song lyrics was a common occurrence.

"Lord, I'm leaving this in Your hands," I said to myself.

My mom and I had to wake up early the next day, as we had to drive over two hours to drive to Duke Eye Center. The ride there was smooth, but I felt a little nervous because I kept thinking about the news I would get based on the results of the futuristic eye exam. When we arrived at our destination, my mom bought me a coffee to give me energy. I drank it while I waited to be seen by an eye doctor, savoring every drop of the bitter yet sweet taste. Finally, when my name gets called, my mom escorts me to the room. I can't remember the exact details of what happened, but the eye doctor kept asking me questions about my vision, my eye pain, etc.

Then a standard eye exam took place. This routine eye exam would occur three more times before I received the news that the light perception in my eyes had decreased, and nothing could be done about it. I dealt with four different eye doctors with four different personalities and bedside manners. One had a warm, gentle voice with a sweet disposition. The other eye doctor was nice enough, somewhere between delicate and demanding, and another eye doctor was a little cold. I can't even remember what the final eye doctor was like. There might not even have been a fourth eye doctor. I'm obviously getting older.

"I feel the heat from the light," I said during one of the eye exams.

"I need you to tell me if you can see it," an eye doctor demanded.

I was also advised to wear sunglasses to prevent debris of any kind from entering my eyes. I also discovered that I have microphthalmos, an eye condition where the eyes get smaller and smaller over time.

My heart sank. My mood changed from relatively okay to complete sadness. "If all of my light perception leaves me, what will I do?" I thought.

There would be no need to look forward to daylight savings time anymore because I would no longer be able to see the literal light of day. I enjoyed viewing the sunshine outside because its light brightened my day and often made my sometimes-sad moods brighter. If my light perception disappears, what will brighten my mood then? Would I be confident walking from place to place? I had so many unanswered questions, questions I never verbally asked anyone. I wanted to cry right there in the eye doctor's office.

"Don't cry in here," my mom said. "Wait to cry in the waiting room." She said something to make me laugh, and I did.

Eventually, we walked out of the eye doctor's office and into the waiting room. The cool temperature hit my skin. Its vast space accommodated all the people waiting to see doctors.

I burst into tears in front of everyone. I was in shock from the news. Before the event that led us to the eye doctor, I would lose my light perception for thirty seconds, and then it would return. It didn't happen too often, but it happened often enough that I could remember those times. But this time, I had to keep in mind that some of my vision had already left, and I feared it would all eventually vanish.

A woman and her family saw what was happening and said, "I'll pray for you. We'll all pray for you."

Though this act of kindness made me feel better, I was still dealing with the shock of the news. Mom kept encouraging me, telling me that everything would be okay, that God would see me through this ordeal. He did see me through this situation and many other trying times in my life.

"Trust in the Lord with all your heart; do not depend on your own understanding. Seek His will in all you do, and He will show you which path to take." Proverbs 2:5-6 (NLT)

I remember the start of 2017. My third year of grad school was quickly approaching. I look at my syllabi. The feeling of nervousness loomed over me. Out of all the classes I was about to take during my sixth semester of grad school, the Clinical Assessment course was the most intimidating. The fear that I might accidentally misdiagnose someone really tugged at me, not to mention a professor would teach the class that I didn't even know. I thought, "What if this professor doesn't like me? What if I fail this class?" I decided to just relax and trust God through the courses.

I met my professor for the Clinical Assessment course, and I really liked her. She seemed fun, and she made the class so engaging with her enthusiastic personality. She turned the boring DSM-5 into a fascinating read. We were even given a workbook to help diagnose people with disorders. The PowerPoint presentations helped me to understand what I should do.

Then the Research Methods course intimidated me too, but I knew the professor. I visited her office when I needed her advice. Although I was doing well in all my classes, I still had to do the internship that I participated in three or four times a week. I was a mentor for youth with disabilities in the K-12 system. As an MSW candidate, I did feel fulfilled. However, there was still something missing from my life. So one night in my apartment, I am sitting at my desk just pondering over my day. I had completed my internship hours, studied class materials, and attended class. Then I noticed that God's word wasn't even being studied.

"You're writing all these papers, studying all these exams, mentoring people, and completing classwork," God said to me. "Where does reading My Word fit in?"

"I know I have to do better," I thought.

Where do I start? There was a time when reading the word of God was overwhelming and terrifying at the same time. The Bible has sixty-six books, many of them consisting of several chapters. So on top of the goals I was already in the middle of accomplishing, I was tasked with figuring out how to make time for reading God's word. Faith was what I needed to get through this.

"Lord, what should I read first?"

"Start with Genesis."

So, that's what I did. I read chapters of Genesis before I started my day. I would read other books in the Bible before bed. A friend invited me to attend a virtual Bible study. Actually, I was volunteered, but I said I would attend it anyway. I wanted to have a closer relationship with the Lord. I also desired for reading God's word to become second nature. I would be an active participant in something without being prompted to do it and without thinking about it. I asked God to help me in this area, and that's what I did.

A year later, I graduated from grad school on Friday, December 8th. That day was a cloudy day, full of rain and cold air. Mom and I drove to UNC Pembroke in all that nasty weather. We even picked up a dear family friend to attend the graduation. When we got out of the car, one of the on-campus police officers walked me into the gym, the cold rain falling on my cap as we strode down the parking lot and onto the sidewalk.

Once inside, Dr. Aiken told us all where to line up. I had my hood draped over my arm as I lined up. However, someone noticed that my cap wasn't on my head the way it was supposed to be. I'll have to thank my crocheted braids for that. Fortunately, there was a spare graduation cap that fit my head perfectly. After someone placed it on my head, we walked to the Givens Performing Art Center (GPAC). Despite the cold and rain, everyone seemed happy.

All the hard work and long nights sitting at our

laptops trying to painstakingly write papers and put together a class presentation paid off. The seemingly endless days we all spent studying for exams we thought we would never pass all paid off. I say all this to convey this message.

No matter what life throws at you, please don't give up. I remember going to grad school asking myself if I was even cut out for it. "What am I doing here?" I asked myself. "I don't belong here. I'm the only blind MSW student, and no one has any idea what it's like to be me. I should just go on back home."

A few weeks into grad school, I called my mother and told her those words. Then, with tears in my eyes, I told her I didn't think I had what it took to make it through grad school. It all seemed so overwhelming. All I wanted to do was go home.

"Daria, if you come home, what will you do? What are your alternatives? You keep going." My mother encouraged me.

So, I did. I kept persevering. I rode the emotional waves grad school would take me through. I also consulted a friend and revealed to her how I felt.

"Don't quit," she said.

I had a withdrawal slip in case I thought I'd need to fill it out, but I never did.

Grad school taught me a lot of things about myself. First, it taught me that I needed to approach how I managed my time. Despite what society had to say, I needed to put my all into whatever I decided to do while putting my best foot forward.

It also taught me that I had people in my corner who believed in the Holy Spirit. My professors, mom, and my friends prayed for my success, perhaps during times when I had no idea they were praying on my behalf at all.

Because I persevered through grad school with the help of the Holy Spirit, I became a mentor for youth with disabilities in the I-12 system. Along with some other friends of mine, I educated them about the importance of self-advocacy and how we had to develop those skills to make it through college. In addition, I assisted the Care Resource Center in researching the impact of food security and homelessness on college campuses, including UNC Pembroke.

When Hurricane Matthew devastated Robeson County in 2016, I was able to help pack hygiene bags and distribute needed items to people who truly needed them. I made a lot of incredible memories. I saw a budding musician in on-campus concerts twice, and I met friends who would help me get through grad school. I even got accepted into Phi Alpha. God is awesome, and I know He got me through grad school.

When I graduated from grad school, I was on cloud nine. My family, friends, and church supported me and celebrated my accomplishment. We took a lot of pictures. Then, for a month, I was really able to relax.

I enjoyed the gingerbread house session we have every year, and I got to enjoy the rest of the holidays.

However, once that month ended, I felt lost. I didn't know what to do next. I got other people to help me write and edit my resume, and I applied for a few jobs, but nothing came of the job leads. It even took a while for me to get my provisional license. That was all my fault. Eventually, I would acquire the license, but I still found I had trouble obtaining stable employment.

During this period, I experienced so much. My mom got into a wreck that could have taken her life. My brother passed away, and Hurricane Florence came and decided to wreak havoc in Southeastern North Carolina. All these events happened within a short amount of time. I had never experienced so much weariness in my life.

Things started to feel overwhelming for me. I didn't care much about finding employment because I didn't want to do much. I was extremely depressed, yet I was in denial about it. I'd be in my pajamas with no desire to get dressed. I would spend time emotionally eating to cope with all the challenges life threw at me during that time. When I put on clothes or even bathed, they felt like chores I had to complete.

On the days I read scripture, I found that I could put on clothes, brush my teeth, and bathe. Despite those trying times, God was still with me. When I felt weary, God, my family, and friends provided me with the strength to move forward with life.

The right to heal.

Yes, we all have that right. We have the right to heal from society's views of us, the right to heal from trauma, and the right to heal from the decisions we made or failed to make. We have the right to heal other people with our laugh, smile, encouraging words, and our presence. My friend described my presence as healing and peaceful. I never thought of my presence as healing. Peaceful maybe, but not healing.

What does it mean to heal someone? To me, healing someone is the ability to make someone feel better. Someone, perhaps a close friend, feels sad. You see her frowning face and think, "What can I do to make her feel better, to cheer her up? I'll say a funny joke or say an encouraging word."

As a social worker, I seek to make the lives of people with disabilities better. I want them to see themselves as achievers and go-getters because society has often told us we were not. Society told us to stay at home because they believed we were way too ugly, hauled us away in institutions so that they could say they had done what they had to do for us. A group of radical disabled people started fighting for our right to live in this world by remaining in a building for twenty-six days until Section 504 was signed. The ADA was not far behind. In a way, the healing process started.

Kamille Richardson

A Mother's Love

I've been asked so many times over the years, "Kamille, when are you gonna write that book?" My answer was always the same. "Book… what book?" I'm just living my life like everybody else. You see, I was born blind—no big deal. At least, that's how I felt. However, the more I thought about it, the more I realized that it was absolutely a big deal! I've had my share of challenges and just as many triumphs throughout my life. Allow me to share a chapter of my story with you. It's pretty amazing if I do say so myself!

Growing up there were never any limitations placed on me. My mother was determined to make sure that her little girl would live a full and happy life, although she would never see the world around her. She didn't shelter me or treat me like I was made of glass.

I played outside with my siblings and other neighborhood kids without a care in the world. I even climbed a few trees in my day! Can't was not in my vocabulary because my mother didn't allow it to live there. She was my biggest cheerleader, and she was always constantly challenging me to try new experiences. I was in all kinds of extracurricular activities, from singing in the chorus to running track. I was perfectly fine with singing in the chorus. I was quite the songbird. Now that track team part, that was all my mother's doing! One day she just up and told me, "Mille, you're gonna be on the track team. I already talked to the coach."

Now y'all, I'm not an athlete now, nor was I then. My first thoughts were, "I'm doing what? And you talked to who? I don't run unless somebody is chasing me!" She made me promise to give it a chance, and if I didn't like it, at least I can say I tried. Of course, I ended up loving it just like she knew I would! My mother instilled in me that not only was my black beautiful, but my blindness was also equally as beautiful.

My sister, Lakila, also played a major role in my life, especially during my childhood and teenage years. I gained a lot of my social skills from her. We shared a room from the time we were babies until we graduated high school. We spent countless hours making up games, songs, and funny stories. We kept my mother entertained, especially when we were in the car.

My sister would make up silly songs about what she saw as we were riding down the street as a way of describing the scenery to me! I wasn't her little blind sister. I was just Mille to her. Our imaginary childhood adventures eventually became real-life adventures as adults. Her belief in me equaled my mother's. They understood me on an intuitive level. They sometimes saw gifts in me that I couldn't see in myself. It is their love and support that would sustain me through trying times.

Although I was surrounded by love and support, doubt and insecurity seemed to lurk around every corner. I couldn't see it, but I knew people were constantly staring at me. I felt like a specimen under a microscope at times! I was someone to be observed but not truly seen. These insecurities began to plague me hard during my teenage years into my young adulthood.

My blindness became my secret shame. Nobody knew my true feelings because I hid them well behind my bubbly, outgoing personality. I presented as well adjusted. I appeared to be handling my challenges with ease and confidence. I never shared my inner struggles with anyone. Not even my mother and sister. I was determined not to show my weakness.

I felt even more ashamed because I was so blessed to have family and friends who never discouraged me and always spoke affirming words over me. Yet, these awful thoughts were my inner dialogue. "You do realize you're blind." "You're not as capable as everybody thinks you are." "You've never seen yourself in the mirror, so how do you know you're beautiful?" "You're gonna let everybody down." These toxic thoughts would follow me around and keep me running from my gifts for years to come.

Ever since I was that carefree little girl I spoke about earlier, I knew I would be a radio personality. I would create shows complete with music, commercials, and my sister as my special guest for every show. I sang in countless talent shows and choirs. I was the queen of the alto section. I was also blessed with the gift of perfect pitch.

This is the ability to recognize the key of a note or song by ear. I eventually began to shy away from singing. I had convinced myself that people only saw me as "that blind girl who could sing" and nothing more. I stopped going out for solo parts because I just wanted to blend in with the group and not have my blindness on display.

I put that beautiful gift of a singing voice up on a shelf. I only took it down in the safe space of the shower or around the house. I told myself that I was going to prove to everybody that I'm more than just a "singing blind girl." The toxic thoughts had won that battle, and I gave them all the ammunition.

I graduated from college with a degree in broadcast communications and landed that dream spot as a radio personality. I was at the top station in my hometown. The one I grew up listening to! I was on top of the world. Or so I thought. Everybody loved me! Nobody cared that I was blind! The listeners didn't know because they couldn't see me!

I was finally flourishing in the gift that is my voice!

Do you know that saying that if something is your passion, you'll do it for free? Well, that was exactly what I did for years while I was working on the radio. I didn't have the confidence or the skills to advocate for myself and the gift that is my voice. I left radio and enrolled in massage school, which shocked everyone and me. I mean, I didn't eat wings or ribs because I hated getting my hands dirty. Now I'm talking about getting a job that requires me to touch people? Ok, sis!

Massage school was a breeze. I passed all my classes with flying colors. I was sooooo depressed though. I felt like a failure. I took the easy way out. I didn't fight hard enough for my true passion. When the instructors asked why we chose massage, my honest answer was, "I don't know."

I was on a winding path, and I had no idea where I was going. But my family and friends stuck by me. They were still cheering me on and lifting me up along the way. I'm sure I was dead weight at this point. Depression and anxiety had become my constant companion by now.

I received my massage license and got a job shortly after. That was the quickest I had found work in the history of my adult life. Blindness was seen as a kind of superpower in the massage world! Hard eye roll!

I lost count of how many clients, managers, and fellow therapists would tell me that this job was tailor-made for me because I had to use my sense of touch.

I would inform them that I had to go to school and get a license, just like my fellow sighted therapists. On the one hand, I was happy because I was earning a paycheck at last! I was living on my own and holding it down all by myself! Go me!

On the other hand, I was still in the throes of severe depression. The feelings of inadequacy still haunted me daily. I was a talented massage therapist, but I knew I wasn't operating in my true gift. Massage didn't bring me joy, nor did it feed my soul. I didn't realize at the time that my gift was still there and shining brightly in those dark rooms.

Clients were constantly complimenting me on my beautiful voice. Some of them even suggested that I should be on the radio! I just shook my head and chuckled! If they only knew. My co-workers would tell me it sounded like a party was going on in my room because I kept my clients laughing. I shrugged off the compliments per usual. That stupid spotlight just wouldn't go away!

It began to get more challenging to get out of bed and go to work every day. I was having trouble functioning in general. My carefully crafted armor was beginning to crack. I slept for hours at a time. There were nights that I didn't sleep at all. My appetite was non-existent. I struggled with these symptoms off and on for years, never recognizing them as severe depression. Then came the panic attacks. They would hit me out of nowhere with an iron grip.

I shared a bit of what I was going through with my family but not all of it. For some reason, I still felt the need to hide the whole terrifying truth. I couldn't tell them about the times I spent in the bathroom at work gasping for air and willing myself to get it together, casually splashing my face with water and getting back to my next client of the day. I didn't want them to worry about me.

Eventually, my truth was laid bare when an ambulance showed up at my house to take me to the hospital, followed by a seventy-two-hour hold. That was the darkest and scariest time for me. How in the world could I let things get this out of control! My family was shocked and devastated, which made me even more ashamed. How could I not lean on them? All they ever did was love me! How did I not trust them when they never gave me any reason not to! How in the world could I hurt them so badly! Finally, I had hit rock bottom, which meant there was nowhere to go but up.

I was determined to get myself together. I started by telling my parents and my sister everything. There were no more secrets. I told them about the years of insecurity, feeling less than like I wasn't enough. I told them that this was all my doing. It had nothing to do with them.

It was a lot for them to digest, but they listened quietly without judgment. They did as they had always done. They loved me through it. My next step was to find a therapist. I finally realized that this situation was bigger than me, and I couldn't fix it without help. Now therapists aren't one size fits all. There was plenty of shopping around to find a good fit.

I cut my work hours to part-time. I spent the time I wasn't massaging working as an independent living instructor for the blind. Many of the clients I worked with weren't born blind like me. They were often terrified of this new and unknown world. I was beginning to operate in my gift once more but in a different capacity.

By simply showing up, guiding them, encouraging, and empowering them, their confidence grew. I loved watching my clients gain new blind skills that came so naturally for me. My confidence increased as well. I began to realize my purpose! I'm a motivator! I speak life into people and pour into them. I show up as the example that blindness isn't living in the dark! I decided to use my voice to empower my blind peers, especially those who lost sight later in life. I was still a massage therapist, but my focus was more precise.

I had become a bit of an expert in technology, especially the iPhone and Apple products. I was the go-to person for most questions, and I found myself teaching individual and group sessions. I eventually became a vendor with my state agency for the blind, and iSee Technology was born! I was a whole entrepreneur in these streets! I was also still working, teaching daily skills, and accepting motivational speaking gigs. I was in therapy on and off but not fully committed. I could feel the old anxiety and depression start to creep back in. No worries. I knew what to do this time. My piecemealed therapy sessions gave me the skills I needed to handle them. I never could've imagined what was to come.

Cancer? Cancer? There is no way I just heard those words straight from the doctor's mouth about my mother! Not MY mother! That can't be! But I knew it was before she said it. I knew it months before we even got here. I felt it in my spirit. People don't just lose thirty pounds in three months for no reason. Hearing it spoken out loud shook me to my core! I wanted to snatch those words out of the air and throw them out the window. I wanted to throw the doctor out the window! But all I could do was sit on that hard cold chair, hold my mother's hand, and will the tears not to fall. I had to be strong for her. She didn't cry, so neither would I.

There was no time for tears anyway. There was way too much to be done. My mother had stage two cervical cancer. She took care of so many people. She was a CNA for years. Unfortunately, she didn't include herself in that group. Treatment was swift and acute. My sister moved in with me for three months while my mother went through rounds of chemo and radiation. By December of 2018, she was in remission. Whew!

We made it through the storm!

Shortly after my mother's diagnosis and treatment, I met the therapist who would change my life. I was drowning again. The water threatened to pull me under and close around me, and I felt powerless to stop it. I had just enough strength to drag myself to the shore and collapse on the bank.

I didn't know what to expect when I walked into her office, but I was desperate for help. My last therapist had ghosted me, leaving me traumatized and untrusting. Michelle's presence was soothing immediately, and we hadn't even sat down. She was an angel! I truly believe it! She seemed to listen with her whole being while I talked. Her questions showed me that she was paying attention. She gave me homework that included exercises that helped me process my thoughts. With Michelle's guidance, I began to live and appreciate my life as I never had before. I spent nine months working through layers of angst, fear, and pain in her office. I felt reborn at the end of our time together.

Finally, I was armed with the tools to battle those toxic thoughts that plagued me for so long! I walked with my head held high with a determination to break chains by continuing to use that God-given gift of a voice. I treated myself to voice lessons! I wanted to sing without abandonment for the first time in years!

My eleven-year massage career came to an end on March 15, 2020. The Covid-19 pandemic was upon us, and states were shutting down left and right. When I walked out the door of the spa that day, I knew I wouldn't be returning. It was time for me to operate fully in my gifts and exercise my faith. I even let my massage license expire for good measure. I couldn't give myself the chance to go back to being unfulfilled. I had been preparing for this for years!

The moment I said yes to my gifts, God began to open doors. He placed people in my life who would be instrumental in this next phase. iSee Technology has grown from providing assistive technology instruction to including diversity and inclusion consulting for small businesses and corporations. In addition, I'm bringing blindness awareness to the sighted!

I dedicate this chapter to my beautiful mother, Jacqueline Bowens. Jackie as she was affectionately called. Unfortunately, her cancer returned, and she gained her wings on the Fourth of July 2021. That date fit her perfectly because she was such a firecracker! The life of the party. There are no adequate words to describe the pain of losing your mother, so I'm not going to attempt to try.

Two months of grief counseling with my angel therapist Michelle helped me survive it. She may not be here with me on earth, but she is forever with me in my heart. She's up there still cheering me on, encouraging me, loving me from afar. She gave me that final nudge to write my way to healing.

Krystle Allen

My Collage of Healing

The journey we travel is not always easy, but who's to say we weren't built for this challenge? I am a proud native of Newark, New Jersey. But my journey doesn't just begin here. My cultural foundation expands from the motherland to the Grand Cayman Islands to a republic in Central America, Honduras. I just so happened to land in Jersey. There's nothing like a good ole Jersey girl.

What a journey already, ain't that right? I think I was a butterfly in my other life because the spirit I hold in my vessel flutters from one place in time to the next.

May 29, 1984, I came in with the storm, baby! Every Memorial Day weekend, there is some kind of storm, overcast, or a chance of something weather-related. Metaphorically, I interpret my arrival with the Latin term carpe diem, also known as *seize the day*. I continue to do just that. At two pounds and fourteen ounces, no doctor could predict a being as small as a bag of sugar would sprinkle sweetness around this place we call the world.

Sometimes I would walk up to random strangers

and express I love them. Innocence is so pure. I feel like I have some magnetic forcefield that just draws people my way. I call it my people power.

Compassion must start with self, especially when you are in a state of moving toward a healing place from a suffering state of mind. You must feel free enough with yourself to elevate your spirit. Far from my apex, I know I am manifesting a solid foundation. I'm the proud eldest of seven siblings, five nephews, and one niece. These generations of life are links representing my inner strength.

Skin Deep

My skin has taken my personality through various life changes. Starting with eczema, it's a noncontagious skin inflammation. It's also referenced as asthma on the skin. I was filled with such discomfort in my skin. Can you believe it? Skin is something you have to live with for as long as you're alive. I just could not grasp my comfort level. I was tormented by the itchiness, teasing at school, depression, low self-esteem, and suicidal attempts. Yes. Suicide, y'all.

I know you are all saying, "How could her skin condition drive her to suicide attempts?" I emphasize the word attempt as defining moments I thought I was so depressed that I did not want to live. I was so young, and I knew that I possessed characteristics people could be drawn to. I could not fathom why it was wrong for me to be dark-skinned or even have a skin condition. Why did something I couldn't control make me ugly to people who did not know me? Why did grown adults tell me I would look so much better if I were lighter? If I could keep a smile on my face, if I had AIDs because my skin was itchy, or if I was burnt because my complexion was richer than theirs. It took me a long while to recognize my power.

I had eczema since the age of five. I think I had every treatment under the sun aiming for some relief for my skin to heal—ultraviolet treatment, bathing in oatmeal, tar solutions, drinking disgusting blood-purifying teas, etc.

A day came when I met a dermatologist that changed my life forever, Dr. Michael E. Jackson. At sixteen, I began treatment with the dermatologist. The confidence I thought I would never experience was shocking to me. For the first time, at sixteen, I wore shorts comfortably. I was not afraid of people seeing my skin. My self-conscious behavior decreased when boys walked by. I went from walking with my head down routinely to walking with pride because my skin was healed, or so I thought. Little did I know, my situation was not my final destination.

Within a year, I went from being overjoyed looking at my clear skin to wondering if I would continue looking with my very own eyes. Vision can be a funny thing. I hated looking at my skin, but I could no longer see its details. It became a major concern.

Post-treatment from Dr. Jackson included excruciating headaches, a year of in and out hospital visits, twenty-two spinal taps, two eye surgeries, and a temporary shunt in my brain. My neuro-ophthalmologist determined seven out of the twenty-five medications prescribed by Dr. Jackson contained tetracycline. Conclusively, the treatment received under his care soon became identified as malpractice. This led to a diagnosis called Pseudotumor Cerebri and Bi-lateral Optic Atrophy. This condition was a rare diagnosis at age sixteen.

During the early years of the millennium, most people who experienced it were in their late thirties or early forties, overweight, consumed high salt intake in their diet, and carried out high levels of stress. Oddly enough, I was a sixteen-year-old, weighing one-hundred forty-three pounds and not having any previously mentioned health issues.

After careful investigations, my Neuro Ophthalmologist learned the root of my condition in reviewing my prescription history. My body responded as an overdose. I had headaches every day for months. They were so severe periodically I could not turn my neck, lift my head, or walk without feeling as if I was going to fall. This condition's activity can include excessive fluid around the brain, optic nerves, and spine. Everyone has what is called cerebral spinal fluid. It is a major element that protects our brain and balances the equilibrium. Normal cerebral spinal fluid levels in any individual should not exceed 12-16 fluid CC's. In my case, fluid levels would rise to thirty-six or thirty-eight. Left untreated, most patients can experience fatal aneurysms. Thankfully that was not my outcome.

I had a rough beginning with this condition, from the uncertainty and speculations from my family members. Nevertheless, I looked forward to starting my junior year of high school at Passaic High. I worked at a gift shop where my mother was employed at the time in a local hospital known as Columbus Hospital.

I knew I was hot stuff. I had a little pocket change coming in from my little summer job. I was looking forward to entering my junior year for various reasons. First, I would be eligible to take a class to secure my driver's permit. Next, I would be able to enjoy the pleasures of public school and sporting my own fashions minus the likes of Catholic school uniforms I wore from K-9th grades.

There was a different plan in store for me. Born and raised in Honduras, Central America, my grandmother was and always will be my ace. However, the Latina Caribbean blood she has can be a pill to swallow at times. I was extremely fatigued with severe headaches before my diagnosis. My grandmother thought I was pregnant initially.

She sternly said to me with her accent, "We're going to see what's really going on."

I thought to myself, "Grandma, don't you have to

have sex to get pregnant? The only woman I ever heard of that gave birth without the act of sex was the Virgin Mary."

Ultimately, after two visits to Irvington General Hospital, they provided my diagnosis. The first eye physician that examined me in that hospital determined my eyes were inflamed. I would have to return to his care within two weeks to be fitted for prescription eyewear. He also prescribed some eye drops to reduce the swelling.

The headaches, sleeping, and confusion about what was happening to me did not provide any answers. As a result of that experience, my grandmother took me back to the hospital. Once we arrived, a different eye physician was on staff, and he performed a more thorough exam on my eyes.

By the end of the visit, he determined I was experiencing pseudotumor cerebri. Not only does this condition produce excessive fluid, but it exhibits symptoms of a brain tumor minus the actual tumor. The excessive fluid causes head pressure. Why is too much water in the head identified as head pressure? Water carries weight in the head.

If you ever experience pain anywhere on your head or in your face, it is identified as head pressure. Abnormal levels can cause constant headaches. It transmits to the brain to press on the optic nerves. It can rupture the optic nerves. It is called papilledema, which will cause the eyes to bulge out of the sockets due to eye swelling from the pressure of the fluid.

However, we all have a skull. It acts as a barrier to the brain when the excess fluid shifts the brain forward to the optic nerves. It realizes it cannot push forward any further then shifts back to the beginning of the spine. This can affect the imbalance of the equilibrium, affecting stability in standing and the ability to walk straight or run without collapsing.

I experienced all of this and more. I spent a year in and out of the hospital to receive treatment. I spent two weeks in ICU hooked up to catheters running from my head to my spine. I was just going through the motions of treatment. I still had eczema despite it all.

You know what? I said vision is funny, right? So is power. It took me some time to digest it all in various settings. Once I began my slow rise like a phoenix, I stepped into my power little by little. My diagnosis was no longer going to overpower my spirit and my life's journey. As a child, I struggled with my identity of self-confidence, inclusion, and self-acceptance because of eczema.

I once was an assertive advocate, sharing my truth with each person I crossed paths with. I was cluelessly broken before my renewed vision. Initially, I did not have much time to adjust to my vision loss. I had to repair my thoughts as I began the figuring out stage of what my life would actually amount to.

I was not familiar with anyone who was blind before. I did not know what resources were available to me to achieve success. Even during an uncertain transition, it's never too late to be whoever you want to be. Twenty-one years of renewed vision has had its challenges, but the reward includes the blessings of the lives I continue to connect with.

Along the way, people and experiences have wanted to place the spirit of defeat and failure in my path. I claim the power of determination and resilience. We are the CEO of our lives. When we are faced with challenges, we should not cancel ourselves. We owe it to ourselves to rise to the occasion. If I had allowed my life before blindness to capture my essence, I probably would not have clutched on to what will be my evolution.

Life After Blindness

I began the figuring-out stage. Adjusting to vision loss is continuous. I went from perfect vision to seeing light and hand motion out of my left eye to extremely blurred vision in my right eye. Out of my peripheral with laser red blinking floater dots in both eyes, is what I have been navigating the world with.

I returned to high school with most of my education spent home-schooled when my condition became overwhelming. I was still a teenager after all, but I was still the eldest out of my siblings. The most important job I have ever had in my life was being the eldest. It was important for me to maintain my ability to be someone they could continue to look up to. I wanted to be able to continue to walk to the store with them, go to the movies, go out to a restaurant, and just be what the big sister can be to her younger siblings.

"Sisters and brothers just happen. We don't get to choose them, but they become one of our most cherished relationships."
-Wes Adamson.

There is Christopher, Courtney, Nicholas, Kayla, Noah, and Aaron. I had a role in watching all their growth up until this very day. They are my motivation to keep pressing forward.

Reflecting on my senior year of high school, I applied for my first job post my vision loss. During this time, my physical vision was stronger. I did not grasp the full benefit of using a white cane and orientation and mobility techniques. I thought it was silly because I could still see a lot. I honestly thought my mobility instructor's job title was ridiculous. I thought he was weird. That was my ignorance of the tools that enrich a visually impaired or blind person.

When I was ready to return to work, you better believe I used my cane skills. I was so proud of my seasonal job at Old Navy. The discounts in the Banana Republic and the Gap retail stores weren't bad either. I would go to class in the day and catch an hour-long bus ride to Jersey Gardens Mall in Elizabeth, New

Jersey, to work as a greeter and floor worker during the evening, stocking the merchandise.

I was beginning the phases to reclaim my authentic self. My parents and older family members were so overprotective of me. I know it was all out of love. It felt smothering at times. After all my steppingstones, my grandfather used to drive me crazy when we would eat out at a restaurant. He would cut my food up in actual shapes. Squares were his favorite for some reason.

I thought to myself, “Why does my food have to be in shapes?” It felt as if my family was having a more difficult time adjusting to my vision loss than I was initially. There was so much they thought I could not and would not experience in life because of my vision loss.

I was home so much that I secretly started taking steps of independence with my six-year-old brother Nick. I would test the waters to sort out my limitations. For example, I taught my brother how to cross the street without intention because I could not see the traffic lights change.

Therefore, his ability to see and recognize colors helped us get from one destination to the next. Nick was a huge part of my adjustment to vision loss at his tender age. I would listen to music a lot. Tweet’s *Southern Hummingbird* album, Dave Hollister, and Musiq Soulchild would be my go-to escape. I loved singing along to those songs home alone. I noticed that my life changed, but my friends began to change along the journey as well.

When I wanted to go out, friends, especially friends who visited me in the hospital, began not wanting to hang out because my use of the white cane was strange from their perspective.

I felt misunderstood and lonely until a friend introduced me to a chat line one day. She suggested it because I was home alone so often maybe it would keep me company. This was a part of my road to discovering my desires. I would call the chat lines and listen to the intros.

Sometimes the guys would sound appealing. Sometimes they would sound strange, and sometimes they'd be so busy scouting for phone sex they just sounded a mess. When I would frequent the chat lines, I would engage in some worthwhile conversation up until the time came when I met my first boyfriend after losing my eyesight.

We would laugh and talk all the time from dusk until dawn. I think I was so lonely that I was in love with the idea of love without understanding the full meaning of romantic love. I did not think about men not accepting me fully because of my blindness. I did not think about the thoughts of men thinking I would become a burden to them because they thought they would have to take care of me. I did not even think about introducing the men I met off the chatline or outside of it as partners that might never consider me as marrying material.

I really had it in my head that the chatline would be the only way I would begin to meet men because of my inability to make eye contact if I was interested in someone. It was like I just could not shake low self-esteem.

From my discomfort with my skin complexion to my disability, there were countless times when I met men off the chatline and when they realized I was not able to see, they acted as if they were going to get something out of their car and would never return. They would ghost me. I thought if I held conversations to get to know them and vice versa after some time, meeting in person would just be easy. Sometimes I would not always disclose my disability until we met, and sometimes not even then.

Sometimes if they paid attention enough, eventually, I would be figured out. Then I would hear responses like, "Are you blind?" Then an awkward silence or peculiar response of hesitance would eject from me. I was just young and inexperienced. You know I wanted to say young and dumb, right? Hey, but those experiences keep life interesting, serving as learning moments.

Although I became a person with a disability, it did not stop my hopes to be desired by a man in all the ways he could desire a woman. I have a disability, but I'm human, not dead.

After several failed introductions, I had to do

some serious reconstruction of myself. I needed to realize the greatness in my purpose.

Renewed Vision

After graduating high school, I pursued college. I was uncertain of the major to select initially. I knew I was interested in being a servant in communities, helping myself, and helping others. I wonder what my life would have been like if I had gone away to college. Before my enrollment, I needed to sharpen my blindness skills.

I received a taste of what independence could look like. I participated in a sixteen-week program at the Joseph Kohn Rehabilitation Center in Newbrunswick, New Jersey. I increased my skills in the areas of mobility and orientation, independent living, assistive technology, and social engagement.

I met some very influential individuals in the program. One of them actually worked with my mother. It was so ironic that she was praying for me while I was in ICU when she could see. Then, when she began losing her vision, our paths crossed again.

The training center lit a fire in me to continue strengthening my claim toward independence. I applied to a cultural exchange program with an opportunity to travel to Tokyo, Japan, with a non-profit named Mobility International USA. This organization provides experiences abroad for people with and without disabilities who have never traveled to other countries.

When I learned of the opportunity, I proclaimed I was going. Get this, I never traveled to Honduras before that time, but I wanted to go to Japan. There were several steps I secured before being selected. First, I applied and went through a phone interview. Then, I played the waiting game. Finally, after some time, I was notified that I was chosen along with eleven other applicants to be a delegate ambassador to Tokyo, Japan. I was the only one to represent NJ at the age of twenty-one.

I traveled across the equator with strangers to advocate for residents with disabilities and indulge in cultural customs. My family doubted me traveling initially because of my vision loss. However, I was determined to show them my abilities through possibilities. You can just call me today's version of Carmen Sandiego.

I returned two weeks after what was a life-changing experience. It made me realize my ambitions were achievable.

Afterward, I began attending junior college, majoring in social science. Pursuing my education did not come easy. I experienced discrimination, lack of accommodations, and self-doubt. I began to realize I could be an asset in the helping profession.

Simultaneous with my education, I wanted to be employed. I have worked in all capacities since the age of fourteen. I was even a phone actress, AKA a phone sex operator, briefly during some time of my younger adult years. Don't tell anybody, y'all. I just have to have my hands on everything.

I worked nine years in the non-profit sector and six years as a certified substitute teacher for grades K-12. Over the past twenty-one years, I had two and three part-time jobs at once. I still made time for sprinkles of lust, love, and adventure throughout it all.

Krystle In the Making

Realizing the helping field was my passion drove me to continue to work in the non-profit field. I noticed those opportunities did not provide growth in my development as a professional. Many of my employment roles were supportive work titles and not leadership. I wondered when my time to shine would come. What would the purpose of my life truly be? I did not have my plan fully mapped out, but I know it requires hard work and determination. Nothing worthwhile falls in your lap. Sometimes it can be developed during your storm.

One day, I was sitting on the toilet feeling bad for myself. I broke up with a guy. As I was on the throne, I had an epiphany. "Krystle, why are you wasting time thinking about someone who is not thinking about you?" I picked up my phone and called my dear friend Naquela Wright-Prievo. I asked her if she would like to begin a non-profit organization.

We had absolutely no idea about the general operations of a non-profit, but we knew we were going to do something innovative. This led to our renewed vision in officiating our non-profit called Eyes Like Mine, Inc. For the past seven years, our mission has been to share awareness about the abilities and potential of individuals with vision loss through community service initiatives, comprehensive empowerment workshops, and innovative social change awareness events. My daytime employment is with the New Jersey Commission for the Blind and Visually Impaired as the community outreach specialist for all twenty-one counties within the agency.

I am busy professionally, but I am also busy personally. After so much anxiety, I decided to return to college to move forward and empower myself to secure my degree. Cross your fingers for me if you will. Receiving my college degree will be my greatest achievement to date. I will be the first college graduate amongst my siblings, parents, and grandparents, and I am doing all of this while legally blind.

I was told I was not college material. I was told I was not smart enough. I was even told recently I was crazy for returning to college because I am so busy. But, in the end, I possess the power for my success. The Lord created me for greatness, not grief.

My non-profit is my 20/20 vision. Eyes Like Mine, Inc. is a part of my legacy. It is my immortality to the world. When I am long gone, I will be remembered for being "Krystle the Connector." My vision loss was my vision gained to share with the world's eyes like mine.

Cheryl Minnette

The Unseen Realities

One thing I can say for sure, with all certainty, life is not what it seems. At first glance, you think you see it all, but the view you see is quite abstract. What you see is barely scratching the surface; it is kind of like looking out onto the ocean. At first glance you see an endless body of water with Beautiful blue hues. Depending on your vantage point, the view may even be considered breathtaking. As you look a little closer, you will notice the water's surface is glistening in the sunlight. Watching, you will see its movement as it ripples, ever so slightly. Every so often, a wave may appear, curling up causing a dip. Dropping quickly and suddenly, it makes contact slamming down into the water below as the sound resonates through the air. Watching this wonderful dance in nature, you will see the waves' whitecaps appear. The show continues with the wave rolling out as the waters blend back together, becoming one with itself. The water then calms, which returns the surface to a beautiful glistening state.

That's it right there, the point of this whole thing. What you're gazing upon is merely the surface. It is those things deep within, hidden below, the unseen reality that needs to be discovered. To know what something truly is, you must see past the surface and discover what's underneath, Nestled between the layers.

Finding things that are very precious and most exquisite, usually takes more than a simple glance or stare. These things can be hidden so deeply that not even a piercing glare will catch sight of them. Now the beauty of it all is there is always more than what meets the eye. Life is never just about what you see. It is dynamic, multifaceted, and intricate, just like you.

Shattered Cracked or Tapping

Cracking open who we think we are, in order to allow what is within to come out, is not the easiest thing to do. This is because it causes us to become transparent and opens up our vulnerability. With this, we are exposing to the world what we have been keeping hidden away inside of us. Sometimes it takes us having to shatter and rebuild from the inside out, in order for us to truly see ourselves.

You see, tapping into those deeply seated inner layers is where our richness and fullness of bounty resides. We are dynamic, multi-faceted, and unique, just like the depths of the ocean. There is so much we possess within us, that it has yet to be explored and discovered. Some of us are curious enough and willing to go in gently. They will allow a tender tap, tap, tap, and then head up an exploration of their own, but only if it is at their own pace.

Others though, due to life's circumstances, have been cracked wide open, but are terrified of knowing what lies inside. For those that are not ready to look inward and explore their inner self, they will attempt to patch and bandage it up. Their hope is it will be sealed up permanently.

Then there are those who have experienced a trauma of such magnitude, it has completely shattered them. Becoming shattered usually sends people on a voyage that lands them at a crossroad. Here is where they are confronted with two choices. Do I pick up the pieces and construct the new me, OR do I sit on my pile of brokenness and slowly fade away?

I strongly believe that everything we go through in life is designed to teach us something. The challenge we usually have is dealing with the lessons that are devastatingly hard. This can cause us to either not learn the lesson, which means we may have to repeat it, or bury the learning deep inside and not use the knowledge gained.

The Dynamic

As a woman who has a strong relationship with God, I have learned to walk by faith and not by sight. This has taken me some time to learn. I am grateful that I am here to share a part of my life with you. I am sure you have heard people say they are here for a reason. Well I truly believe that without a shadow of a doubt. There were many times on my life's journey when, if it had not been for the grace of God, I would be 6 feet under. I strongly believe there's a divine calling on my life, which allows me to continue to walk this earth. There are times when things happen in your life and you ask God why. Why has this happened to me? Why am I going through this? Why are things the way they are? Sometimes we receive the answer. Other times, no answer is the answer we get.

When a window opens between two worlds, one can be amazed and petrified in the same moment. Seeing what lies within, while being on the outside is simply miraculous. Consciously being in both places at the same time can be mind blowing.

Looking to the right, I saw the world as I knew it to be. Looking to the left, I saw a place I never imagined I would get a glimpse of. It all happened in an instant. Another shift had just occurred. How does this happen with no clue or warning? In that fraction of a second, when the moment of realization hits, your mind can travel a trillion miles away; then Bam! You, now find yourself, right back in the midst of the moment, where the crisis has already begun.

Walking by faith and not by sight, allows you to see the visions of your future.

Strength Knowledge and Power

There was a time in my life when I was drowning and people were just watching it happen. I was no longer singing. I was no longer dancing. A smile or laughter became foreign to me. The things I saw around me were no longer the same. It was as if the people I knew were no longer the people I saw. They appeared different to me, because now their masks were off. What was then revealed, made me feel like I was living in an altered state. Sometimes it takes you to go through a period of devastation, in order to find out who the people are around you.

As I continued to gasp for breath, I remembered I had the power to change my circumstances. I remind myself, I had the power to reclaim my identity. I also realized, I had the power to regain my strength. Having the power to break free from all circumstances that were not divinely ordered for me and not using it, is a waste of a life. Since I'm not someone who gives up on themselves, I shifted my focus upward and onward. Now, don't get me wrong or misunderstand, shifting isn't necessarily easy, but may be necessary in order to save your life.

After surviving an extremely difficult divorce, I triumphantly walked away with the ability to write legal documents. During the process, I paid very close attention and was able to write them so well, I should have added 'Esquire' to my name. You see, I had been living in survival mode for many years, whilst in the midst of a war. Like any war, the objective is to not get hit (by enemy or friendly fire) but rise from the ashes victorious. As God is my witness, victorious I was. I walked away with scars that remained for many years, but I also walked away with my life and my freedom.

Starting over with two young children, a dog, and everything else that came along with it, I was determined to make things work. As time went on, I seem to have mastered juggling everything within the time constraints. During this process, it took a while for the realization to hit me that my role in society had shifted. I was no longer categorized as a married woman. I was now an unwed mother, a single mother, or as some people like to label it, a 'Baby Mama'. The ripple effect of this new status affected our relationships, friendships, and associations. So much to think and strategize about, but not more than I could handle.

Little did I realize, more devastation was rearing its ugly little head. It locked its sight and was looking straight at me. Unprepared and unsuspecting what was about to happen, it came upon me like a thief in the night. It destroyed what I had been building. My life was shattered, once again.

You see, my intention was to be the best role model for my children I could be. While giving them all the love and nurturing possible, I worked on regaining my identity, whilst getting my life back on track. I began harnessing the power I knew I possessed deep within. I created a new routine and had moved forward with it. Everything seemed to be fitting into place, which was work, school, parenting, and the millions of other tasks that are included along with being a single mother.

Wednesday morning was here again, so the routine was pretty much the same. Rise and shine everyone, let's go, let's go, let's go! Escorting our beloved family mascot, Sam (our 10-pound, tan colored Pomeranian), for his final morning walk was always an enjoyable time. After offering Sam our loving farewells for the day, the little ones headed off to school. Once I took a few deep breaths, it was off to work for me.

On that particular beautiful spring morning, everything was going smoothly, right according to plan. I recall strolling across the parking lot, while enjoying the cool crisp morning air. As I made my way through the building, I wondered how busy we would be that day. Moving along at a brisk pace, I quickly neared my destination. Seeing what I had not seen the day before, appeared a bit strange.

As I got closer to my area, I kept seeing a strange looking red all around. This was not the norm, so I became a bit puzzled. Although not yet understanding why I was seeing so much red, I continued walking, looking about and pondering. At some point, I glanced up and stared at the ceiling light, not believing what I may have been seeing. In the moment I stopped breathing, stunned by what I was witnessing.

While catching my breath, I looked all around. Looking to the right I saw the workplace, as it would normally be. Looking to the left, all I saw was red. Never in my wildest dreams did I think I would be allowed to see the inner workings of my eye. I was shocked to realize the red I had been seeing was my blood, as it circulated and flowed through my eye.

That's right, you heard me right! I actually witnessed seeing my own blood, moving internally through my eye. It was at that very moment I lost my breath and time seemed to stand still. I touched my face, expecting to be horrified by seeing my hands dripping with blood. I thank God they were clean. Grateful and bewildered I was not bleeding out, I anticipated pain to kick in at any moment. There was none. No pain, no discomfort, and definitely no warning.

Petrified, and in sheer disbelief, I reached out for something, ANYTHING that would brace me for the ride that had already begun. As I felt panic rising through my body, I began taking deep breaths and focusing my mind, so I could regain mental control. I approached a coworker and began explaining to her what was happening. When her morning smile and facial expression turned to shock and horror, I lost my control. Tears began to flow and I started trembling.

The only pain that I felt during this trauma was post-surgical. I had to undergo multiple surgeries, and the pain was definitely real. My detached retina was able to be repaired, but I was left legally blind. With no warning, no oncoming pain, my eyesight was gone in an instant. The moment this happened was the moment my life came to a hard stop.

It then shifted in ways I could not have possibly imagined. I imagined I would marry once, to a man that would be my life partner, 'til the end. My plan did not come to pass. I imagined I would have good clear eyesight in both eyes, to see my children mature, marry, and have families of their own. Well, I do believe in miracles, so I'm waiting to see what God has in store for me. In life, I have learned the following:

"Plan with God, not without God, because His plan is the master plan."

The Brain Game

Learning those things you cannot do, but you really can do, is like solving a Rubik's cube! You know it can be solved, you know you are capable of solving it, but the challenge is figuring out how to go about it. Enter, the brain game.

Everything that we have ever thought about or experienced in some way shape or form is stored in our brain. Every memory you have ever had, has been organized, categorized, departmentalized and more. The brain is a living resource. Your own personal internal central processing unit. How awesome is that?!

Why am I now talking about the brain? Since losing my eyesight, I have worked extremely hard to maintain my independence. You see, I lost my job, lost my driving privileges, and even lost some friends. With that and everything else, I was still raising my children, caring for a young dog, cooking, cleaning, and all the rest. At some point I realized I might as well toss out all the 'How To' manuals, along with my notes, because they were no longer valid. How I used to do things versus how I will be doing them going forward, was two different processes.

You see, in order to maintain my independence, I had to create strategies and techniques, so I could remain independent while caring for those I love. This occurred both inside and outside of the home. I needed to figure out how to get things done properly, within my new lifestyle. Practice may not make perfect, but it sure comes close.

Figuring out how to manage the details of life was challenging, but doable. I wanted my children to have me in the same capacity with my sight loss, that they had when I was sighted. I still haven't figured out driving yet, but the strategies and techniques I have implemented in other areas are definitely working.

At first, I questioned myself about many things, especially the ones that were special to me. Would I have the ability to still do certain things? For instance, I used to spend time with my daughters styling their hair and having home spa nights. They would get manicures, pedicures, and soothing massages. Guess what? I figured it out and we continued to enjoy those moments! They still smile and get excited when we reminisce about those days.

The kitchen was a whole other beast to conquer. The kitchen is my playground. As a foodie, I love being in the kitchen. I definitely had to retrain my brain in quite a few areas, including organization, storage, and safety. The highest number of kitchen injuries in the blind and visually impaired community are burns and cuts. Safety is major!

I have burned myself and even cut a finger almost clear to the bone. That seems kind of ironic, seeing as how I now have The Cooking Blind Kitchen online show. When you know better, you can do better.

Know that you can do anything you put your mind to. Your brain is designed to work for you, not against you. Tell it what you need, by writing it down. Show it what you want, through visualization. The more you intentionally work with your brain, the better your brain can work for you.

Reflections

Who I used to see in the mirror and who I used to be, is not who I am anymore. When I reflect back on the Cheryl of yesteryear, I see a shattered woman in motion, who was living in a state of tiredness. Have you ever felt like you had no energy and the only thing that kept you going was the fumes of exhaustion? My shoulders were tired from carrying the weight of others. My back was tired from carrying the baggage of life's situations. I was tired of living in survival mode. I was tired of living a stress filled lifestyle. Although I was tired of always being tired, through it all I was still serving others.

I must thank my parents for what they have taught me. I observed their strong work ethic and their compassion for all humanity. I approach life as an adventure of which I am in to win. Yes I lost my sight, job, driving privileges and more, but I never lost hope or the knowledge of my abilities.

It took me a while to understand my new life circumstance. I now know without a doubt, my disability lives with me, I don't live with it. When I step into a space, first you see me (or not), then you meet me and get to know my essence. My sight loss is always present, but it is not in the forefront.

Moving forward in my life, I began to focus on me and how I could make a difference, an impact in this world. I have always been a lover of words, so I knew my writing skills would play a part in this. Whether I'm writing for myself or ghost writing for others, the experience is always enjoyable. I am humbled to have become a best-selling author with more on the way. Although writing is one avenue on which I travel, speaking is another. Motivating and inspiring others to take forward action in their lives is very rewarding.

The daily challenges and victories of my sight loss has allowed me to assist individuals, families, and caregivers, by sharing my knowledge with them. The strategies and techniques I have developed, allow for successful living. Having a roadmap, blueprint, or schematic, whether digital or not, allows one to better maneuver, making their steps more intentional.

"It's not the challenge you have to concern yourself with, it's your approach."

Creating a business and online space was definitely new and challenging for me. Shaking in my boots, I jumped in and was determined to learn what I needed to know. I have worked with some great coaches and mentors. Even came across a few you should definitely stay away from. As a businesswoman, it has been a joy learning the online space and adding to my skill set. Having the ability to empower others to become more than they currently are it's truly a blessing. Life is to be lived, and to do that one must be present in life, not just drifting along.

There were times when I was just drifting through life, trying to maintain my breath. Life had beaten me down so badly I was barely existing. What saved me was my faith, my knowledge of self, and a very dear friend who acted in the moment. Their action and God's grace sent me a lifeline that literally saved my life. I knew I was shattered, although I did not know how deeply, but I also knew I had the right to heal. The thing was, I had to want my healing enough to fight for it. I have fought to survive in the past, but this was different. This time not only was the fight to survive, but I was also fighting to be transformed. This fight was for full healing.

You Are Enough

When it comes to entitlement, everyone has the right to heal from whatever they are challenged with. Healing itself, is a process which takes time. The amount of time needed varies, depending on the individual and their circumstance(s). Healing is not something that just happens, you have to allow it to occur.

I, like you, have the right to heal. Knowing yourself and trusting yourself, is a process that can be learned. Writing can be used as part of one's healing process. Writing is a way of bringing things from the inside out, without speaking a word. This is what makes it such a powerful tool. You are enough and were created to be enough.

You must dig deep to grab hold of your value. Do not blind yourself watching what others are doing, because their works are for them, not for you. We all have our own path to walk. Sometimes there are bricks missing that we must lay ourselves. While laying those bricks, strength and confidence will be built. Allow your positive energy to flow through every part of your being, through your fingertips and across your lips. Exclaim to the world you are here.

"God's future for you is before you. Know when He shows you something, you will have to work to get there, but it is waiting for you and you alone."

Mirranda Williams

Hands of Healing

I am whipped across the behind with a belt. Stay on your knees and call on Jesus until the holy ghost is felt, where it is no wind and too much heat in which you will melt, the dirty South, the peaches, and pecans state! If you haven't guessed it yet, Georgia lays claim to my heart and soul! As a true Southern woman, we must begin with some housekeeping, so listen closely!

First, my family calls me Shonda. When you see this, do not be discombobulated! Second, I can't tell you how to feel when you read my story, but please do not pity me! Lastly, I apologize to y'all!

People, you have been privy to an actress that is proficient at her craft! I have been playing the part of a "bubbly" person for much of my life. That façade hid the demolished spirit of a female. I concealed her with jokes, a smile, and awful decisions.

At this moment, as you read this chapter, I present to you my unapologetic, unmitigated, and uncensored truth. Now that housekeeping is out of the way, please find your designated seats. The train is leaving the station!

The Caboose

You will reap what you sow, but them hands though! I thought I was good with my hands! The funny thing is I was always getting caught! I started stealing when I was around ten years old.

At home, I stole snacks, money, makeup, and anything else I thought would make my family mad or cause them to hurt. Why? Because it served them right! I wanted them to hurt the same way they hurt my feelings. Don't get me wrong. I know my family loves me, but the pain my loved ones inflicted on me verbally and physically was enough to drive me to use my hands.

"Shonda! What have I told you about putting your hands on things that do not belong to you?" When my momma made this statement, I would just look at her and think to myself, "I did it to pay you back for hurting my feelings," or I even went so far as to scream in my head, "Because I hate you!"

Outwardly, I would be crying. Not because I felt remorse but because my plan to make her hurt was not successful. Now, I would have to find something else to steal to make my point.

This same bad habit transferred over into school. The schoolteachers, administrators, and students that I felt needed to feel my hurt was also touched by my hands. I stole stuff from the teachers' desks, from their classrooms, and out of their bags if they were careless enough to leave them out. I stole my fellow students' pencils, pens, books, and even a girl's diary to see what else they were saying about me.

I remember the first time my fifth-grade teacher caught me. I had stolen my grandma's pretty lapel pins and brought them to school to distribute them to a few girls I thought were my friends. One of the girls showed her gift to our teacher, and my misdeed was uncovered.

On that day, one week before Christmas, I Mirranda, AKA Shonda, was labeled a thief by nearly the entire school, but did I stop stealing, though? The better question would have been, did they realize how much their bullying hurt me just because I was partially blind?

Hindsight is 20/20

If I had seen this coming, you could bet your bottom dollar that I would have avoided it! Who gets in trouble for stealing their own clothes out of the house? I did. That's who. My granny supervised us when it came to going anywhere important. This includes our school routine.

In the fall of 1999, Central High School really enforced the school dress code. Did Eudell care? Not at that time. She had already bought our school clothes. The school system did not give her any money, and they were not going to tell her what her grandchildren could wear. I digress!

Picture It. –Sophia, *Golden Girls*

A young girl is about to embark on the journey of her life! Her body has filled out into a voluptuous, bodacious black beauty (at least in her eyes) on her way to catch the bus bearing down the neighborhood street.

The young beauty is stopped from leaving by her disgruntled grandmother. She grabs her backpack and rifles through it. The beauty begins to tear up when she realizes that her secret has been discovered. Her grandmother gives her the eye that says "you are in trouble" without her mouth uttering one single word as she yanks the hidden pair of white pants out of her notebook.

Later, as the young girl makes her way through the school halls to reach her homeroom, she is stopped by the principal himself. "Young lady, please come with me." The frightened girl slowly treads behind him because she knows what is going to happen next.

In the words of Sophia from the *Golden Girls,* people, that young girl was me! What happened next was the catalyst to my cross to bear and my blessing.

When I returned home from school that day, I ran

into the house and stayed in my room under the pretense of having a lot of homework to get done. I was hoping that if I sat quietly, I would be out of sight, out of mind. Nope. That did not work in case you were wondering! About seven that evening, Grandma came around the corner with her tool of pain in her hand—a cut-off piece of a water hose. Don't laugh, y'all. That thick piece of rubber hurt! I digress!

I was made to stand to receive my punishment. I did. I thought I took my punishment like a true G until, in my efforts to stop my grandmother from hitting me, I grabbed the water hose. I was pushed back and turned around to be held still between her hand and the wall.

Unfortunately for me, there was a nail at eye level that punctured my eye. I began to scream, "My eye! My eye!"

I think that my grandmother thought it was a ploy to get her to stop administering my punishment. Interestingly enough, my eye did not bleed. However, it looked as if I burst several blood vessels and had pink eye all at the same dang time. Interesting enough, that is what my grandmother claimed happened to my eye.

After that night, I never ironed anything that could cause me to get another beating, such as the one I received that night. So, my life went on as a moody fifteen-year-old, trying to find my place in the world. But little did I know, my world would be turned upside down in a few months!

I did not notice the change in my right eye until after my first blackout. At this point, I had already lost vision in my left eye, but I did not tell my parents. My first blackout took only a few minutes. I blinked my eyes a couple of times, and shortly my sight was restored. I thought my mind had played a trick on me and immediately dismissed the episode.

Funny how we dismiss the direct signs that could be the thing that will make or break us! The second blackout was about the same, but the third blackout... it was a doozy. It took over twenty minutes for my vision to return. It happened while I was running through the halls of Central High, trying to get to my gym class.

Suddenly, everything had gone black. I stopped and stood still, thinking that it was okay. I will just wait this out. Then, at the seven-minute mark, tears begin to roll down my face. While I was standing there, the assistant coach spotted me in the hall.

“Tucker! What are you doing in the halls? Get to class!”

“Coach,” I whispered, but he didn’t hear me over his yelling!

“Move now, or you will run the track for the rest of the period.”

“Coach!” This time, I yelled a little louder.

“What?” he yelled.

“I can’t see,” I cried.

I was escorted to the office and sat in there until my vision returned. This experience shook me enough to know that something was wrong.

The school called my mom and explained what had transpired. My mom said that she would take me to the eye doctor. I went, and the doctor claimed that the blackouts could have been caused by an allergic reaction to something I was putting on or in my eyes.

My grandma claimed that's what was happening because I was known for stealing her makeup, and she was missing a new bottle of mascara that she had just bought. I know what y'all thinking, but nope. I did not have it this time, but once a thief, always a thief, right?

After my last blackout, my vision seemed to improve. I was seeing better than I had before. My vision in my left eye was still gone, but the sight in my right allowed me to continue life as a troubled high school student. It was not until we had gotten out of school for Christmas break that my life would change forever.

It was Christmas Eve. It was time for all the children in the house to go to bed. I remember looking around my room, making sure that it was clean so I would not have to do any cleaning in the morning. I remember looking at my dark rose-pink walls and thinking that I really do not like pink as I walked toward the bathroom mirror.

As I stood primping in the mirror, fussing with my headscarf, I looked down at my light blue pajama set with white clouds on them, thinking they were dorky but cute. Then, I looked back up and stared into the mirror at my reflection, thinking that I wasn't that ugly. On a good day, I could pass for cute.

I remember saying, "God, why do I have to be so ugly that nobody loved me? My father doesn't love me. My mother and grandma always called me names such as fat, stinking woman, blind bat, and much more." I let a teardrop, smiled a little at myself, and made myself a promise that I was going to be somebody someday. I would show them who was not good for anything. With that thought, I walked back into my room, took one last look around, and climbed into bed.

On Christmas Day 1999, I woke up later than everyone else! I jumped out of bed because I heard my grandma's old forty-five playing my favorite Motown hit Christmas song. I was sitting up in the bed singing my little heart with my eyes still shut! Santa clause came down the chimney at half-past three, y'all.

At some point, I opened my eyes because I heard my mom coming through the hall. By the time she had made it to my room, my eyes had been opened for a few minutes. As my mother walked past me, I asked,

"Mama?"

"What do you want, Shonda?"

"Is the light on?"

"Yeah!"

Upon hearing my mother's reply, I closed my eyes unnecessarily because at this point, even with them remaining open, I was still in the dark! Well, merry Christmas to me. It was another blackout, or so I thought.

On that day, my vision left me for good. Nobody knew it for certain, though. How is that possible? It was easy because my entire immediate family had vision problems, so when I ran into things or fell, they did not question it because I had done this all my life. So my loss of vision stayed hidden until the end of February.

Sometime within the last week of February, my deceit was uncovered. One student who recognized that I had lost my vision began leading me around in school by letting me hold on to the loop at the top of his backpack.

At this point, my teacher had started letting me out of my homeroom five minutes before class to avoid the crowds because I had explained to her about the blackout episodes I was having. This day, we did not make it to my first-period classroom before the bell rang.

As a result, he began to run to make up the distance to the building's door before the students began to pour out of the classrooms. I began to run also, and what happened? I ran full force into a portion of a brick wall that was jutting out on my blind side. My face connected with this brick wall and knocked me back on my butt. The students who saw the accident happen began to laugh and call me names, such as a blind bat.

With blood and tears mingling together on my face, I struggled to pick myself off the ground. I dragged into class, sat down, and tried to stop crying, but I was in so much pain. My face was throbbing, I was bleeding, and my feelings were being hurt by the students and their boisterous laughter about the blind, ugly girl who ran into a brick wall. I began to cry harder. Finally, the teacher told me that If I could not get myself together and stop disrupting her class, I could go to the office.

At that point, I screamed out I couldn't go by myself because I could no longer see. That prompted the teacher to ask a student to escort me to the office. I was asked what happened, and the school called my momma. I was told that I was a hazard to myself and others, and I could not return to school until I went to the eye doctor.

He only confirmed what I had already known for months at the doctor's office. "Ms. Tucker, your daughter is totally blind, and I am afraid it is permanent. From what we can tell, she has Secondary Glaucoma, which is caused by an injury to the eye."

After the doctor made that statement, I closed my eyes, and it took nearly two years for them to open again! Several days after that doctor's visit, my family speculated what could have caused my blindness. But the main one that stuck with me was what my grandma told me.

"See, Shonda? All that putting your hands on stuff that did not belong to you... God allowed you to be blind to stop you! Then again, you probably just put your eye out from poking yourself in the eye with my mascara wand. Where is it anyway? You can't use it anymore!"

I replied, "I did not have it."

She called me a liar and a thieving heifer and told me to get out of her face. If y'all are wondering, I really did not steal this makeup. She found it at the bottom of her purse but accused me of dropping it back in there when she was not looking.

The weeks that followed my official diagnosis came and went in a fog. I was extremely depressed, and all I wanted to do was sleep. I barely ate. I did not want to talk to or see anyone. Sometimes I would lie in bed and hold up my hands in my face in hopes that I would be able to see them. All I could think was my hands got me into this mess. If I had not been trying to retaliate and pay people back from hurting my feelings by stealing their stuff, I would not be blind.

I almost gave up.
I was right on the edge of a breakthrough but couldn't see it!
-Kurt Carr "I Almost Let Go"

Along with my blindness came invisibility, the

control and restrictions, and a new school. Since I was now the only person in my family who was completely blind, I thought they would be different. My grandma always used to say that we were good for nothing, and I truly believed so. I could not see, and therefore, there was no reason for me to continue to live. Yes, y'all. I tried to commit suicide several times. My last attempt happened on my first anniversary. I tried to smother myself on Christmas Eve.

Why did I try to kill myself? My family's tradition is to drive through neighborhoods and look at the Christmas lights. We all would load up in the family's royal blue van. As we went by, my other siblings admired the pretty lights and figurines in the yards.

I kept my head turned towards the window in hopes that the Lord would allow me to see some flicker of light. He didn't. I had prayed that He would, and since He went back on His promise to answer my prayer, I felt that He did not love me either. As a result, I sat quietly with tears running down my cheeks, silently battling my heart, mind, and soul. My heart was hurting because no one thought about my feelings. Who was supposed to care and love me? My mind was telling me since they didn't care for me, just to end it once and for all. And my soul was crying out to God and asking Him why I was being forsaken.

After returning, I put on the same blue pajamas with the white clouds I had on the previous Christmas, even though I had gotten new ones. Nobody noticed! I went and stood in the mirror, praying for the Lord to open my eyes. It did not happen! I climbed into bed and buried my face in the pillow while listening to grandma's Motown Christmas Forty-Five. I truly tried to smother myself but stopped at the last minute because I heard a voice whispering to me, "If you kill yourself, how will you know what you are capable of?"

At that point, I believed it was my inner self speaking to me. It was not until I deepened my relationship with the Lord that I understood that He was preparing me for my destiny!

After those words were whispered to me, I began to have a new outlook on life. I was the cause of me being blind from putting my hands on things that did not belong to me.

I thought if I did enough good in the world, maybe my sight would be restored! I started attending church with a purpose, singing from the heart, praying on my needs, and giving things away free to people I saw in need.

It was not until January 2002 that I began to recognize my potential. It was always my job to cut up the veggies for my grandma for any holiday meal. I thought I would get out of it since I was blind. Nope!

"Shonda!" My grandma yelled early one morning. "Get your butt up, wash up, and come in the kitchen."

I did as I was told. Upon entering the kitchen, my grandmother handed me a paring knife and told me to sit at the table.

"What do you want me to do, Grandma?"

"You fixin' to cut up my vegetables!"

"But, Grandma, I can't see!"

"So? Your hands do not have anything to do with your eyes. Take this knife and cut up my vegetables like I showed you, and you better not get any blood in my food either, or I am going to whip your ass!"

Reluctantly, I took the knife and started slicing the veggies into strips as granny had taught me and then cut them into little cubes. By the time I had cut up two bags of celery, ten bell peppers, and one bag of onions, I felt on top of the world. There was no blood in the veggies either.

I don't know if my grandma intended to try and restore my confidence in myself by getting me to do something that I was accustomed to doing, but that was the result.

From that day forward, I began to take control back despite being blind. I refused to let people do something for me if it was within my ability to perform the task independently. Unfortunately, I was labeled a bitter, mean, blind person for this.

However, they were only half right. I was not being bitter because I was blind anymore. I was mean and bitter because the people in my community made me that way. I was constantly stared at because of the disfigurement of my eyes. My left eye had deteriorated and sunk in on itself because of the nail puncture. My right eye bulged because of the built-up fluid and pressure transferred from my left eye. This, I admit, made for a hideous sight, but I did not want to wear shades like Stevie Wonder or Ray Charles. Therefore, I continued to be the one-eyed female cyclops who lived in Macon, Georgia.

Although my blindness was traumatic, I tell people all the time that it was my blindness that was the perfect gift! People, if I had not gone blind, I would have been doing one of three things—in jail, turning around on a pole with twelve children somewhere, or buried six feet under the ground. Going blind stopped all of this.

My blindness allowed me to close my eyes to what was and opened my mind and heart to the possibilities. I am not going to lie to you and tell you that my life has been easy as a blind woman. However, I will tell you that I would not change one thing about my life. With God's help, I am walking by faith and not by sight. The moves I make now are driven by the fact that I am confident in myself as a black, beautiful, bold, blind woman, and no one can take that from me!

It took me a long time to get to this point. Like most women, I have been in horrible relationships, used by men and women alike, and even experienced domestic violence. I have been stolen from and taken advantage of more times than I can count. I charged those experiences to the game. My grandmother told me numerous times I would reap what I sow. And believe me, I did. I had some crazy experiences. I will tell y'all about them in the next *Write 2 Heal,* but for the sake of time, I am going to skip right to the point when I understood that my hands were good for something else than stealing.

I was nineteen years old when I moved from my grandma's house. I loved helping others and wanted something to do besides sitting on my butt at home collecting a check from the government, so I applied to be a volunteer worker at the local McDonald's house. I built up my confidence to call and ask did they need any help. The person on the other end of the phone, after listening to me, excitedly confirmed that I could help there.

"Oh, but wait. I am blind. Is this going to be a problem?"

"Umm, you can still use your hands, right?"

"Yes. There is nothing wrong with my hands!"

"Then I don't see what would prevent you from participating in service projects."

This lady gave me something to live for on that day! Even though I had not fully recognized my full potential, I was able to contribute to this organization in so many positive ways.

At that moment, surrounded by parents needing comfort and companionship, I, the ugly blind girl, could provide these things. I couldn't see, but I was able to use my hands to reach out and hug someone in their time of need.

I was able to reach out my hands to lift someone else from their lowest point. I was able to use my hands to feed someone who needed a home-cooked meal, and most of all, I was able to lift those same hands to God, who saw fit to allow my eyes to be closed so my hands could lift and give Him praise for the many blessings and opportunities that I have had thus far!

Meet The Authors of

The Write 2 Heal

The Visionary
Jeanetta Price

Jeanetta Mary Alice Price is the visionary behind the anthology, *The Write 2 Heal.*

Her mission in life is to help others tap into their vision by utilizing writing as an instrument of healing. Often, she reflects on the life of the virtuous woman, Essie Andrus, her biological and spiritual mother who leads by example with unwavering faith. God blessed Jeanetta with the gift to write to save her life, and she wrote herself "beautifully healed."

A Texas-raised, distinguished star from a little big city called Beaumont, she is a graduate of Lamar University with a bachelor's degree in social work

and a master's degree in clinical mental health counseling. In addition, she is the Founder and CEO of

Blind Girl Magic and a licensed mortgage loan originator known as the "Outta Sight Mortgage Loan Lady."

As a spoken word artist, she hosts The Write 2 Heal seminars that include poets, partner artists, and even audience members who will participate in an open mic session. The seminars provide a safe poetic space for all participants to begin their journey of healing while writing.

The freedom of expression, boldness, vulnerability, and confidence set her aside from other authors, artists, and advocates. Unapologetically, the material written reflects her unique personality, life experiences, social injustice, disability, and social awareness complimented with God-given creativity. The fire that resides in her bones spreads wildly around the atmosphere and set others on fire to stand fearless in their truth as they too write to heal. Yes, Jeanetta was given the vision but could not deliver the birth of this book without the visionaries.

Jasmin Duffey

Jasmin Duffey is a noted spoken word artist, writer, and audio engineer.

Jasmin graduated from MTSU with a bachelor's degree in communications with an emphasis on journalism and broadcasting. She also minored in theatre

She is a consultant with the Shepherd Center in Atlanta, GA, and with AT&T for product development and accessibility for blind and low-sighted individuals.

She is a highly sought-after spoken word artist and has traveled around the US, gracing many stages with her remarkable words. She produces, writes for, and engineers several rising R&B and hip-hop artists

In her free time, she can listen to YouTube, stay current on the world, and study new topics of interest, which are many as she lives to learn.

The author believes resilience is a science to silence the storm in your life and to find healing no matter how hard she hides. Her story *Benched* will leave you laughing through your tears and, in the end,realize the power of resilience and the freedom to heal.

Lynette Eberhardt

The youngest of two, Lynette Eberhardt, AKA Lyn with one N, grew up in the suburbs outside of Cincinnati, Ohio. She used to write short stories and poems that she never let anyone read, afraid to let others know her thoughts. Young Ms. Eberhardt felt like she was a misfit and used her writings to cope. Eventually, she embraced her differences as uniqueness and slowly started to blossom into a confident, determined, strong-willed woman.

Her mother was a God-fearing, strong, hard-working, well-liked, proficient, family-oriented, accepting of everyone, willing to help anyone, the loving songstress who was Ms. Lyn's biggest supporter. Lyn's chapter is in memorial of her mother, Mrs. Linda G. Eberhardt.

Ms. Eberhardt has two associate's degrees, one in accounting technology and the other in business management. She recently received certification to be a peer supporter for individuals with disabilities, focusing on the blind/visually impaired.

Others describe her as down-to-earth, funny, perky, resilient, positive, too kind, loyal, outspoken, bold, and dauntless.

Her hobbies include traveling, reading, writing, spending time with family, advocating for the rights of people with disabilities, making people laugh, and singing—which led her to join The Augusta Chorale in 2015.

Ms. Eberhardt now resides in Augusta, Georgia, and is the mother of a fur baby. She is in training to learn JAWS, the talking computer program, to finish her bachelor's degree and is considering pursuing a career in writing.

Stay tuned…

Samuel JoNita Gates

Since childhood, Samuel JoNita Gates has been a writer and continues this passion now, even in adulthood. Her beginning writing experience for publication was as a weekly article writer for three years for *Garrison in the News.* Gates is a native of Garrison, Texas. Her first published work as a novice author is titled *The Color of My Hair.* Her writings share personal experiences in multiple styles or genres.

Gates is an ordained servant of God, a veteran teacher, a writer, poet, author, and singer. Gates' passion for words and writing extends into the ministry that God has called her to oversee. It is a ministry, spoken and in action, fulfilling the goal and mission statement "Sharing the Love of God by Sharing the Word of God." She is the God-directed organizer and founder of Samuel Gates Ministries Ministering H.O.U.S.E.

H.O.U.S.E. is an acronym that lists or explains the work, mission, and goals of the ministry members.

Gates has also experienced motherhood with three children, Henry, Gregory, and Lola. They have enlarged her heritage of the Lord with ten grandchildren who know her as Grammy.

Continuing the passion, Gates' forthcoming books, *Memoirs of Experiences* and *I Pray, You Pray, We Pray,* are ready for the editor.

Stacie Leap

Stacy Leap resides in Philadelphia, Pennsylvania with her beautiful daughter, Alana, which means "shining star" in Hawaiian. Her daughter and radical faith are why she took a "Leap of Faith."

Overcoming her darkest moments, surviving an abusive relationship, and adjusting to unexpected vision loss, God blessed her with a daughter to help Stacie find her way back to Him, learning to love herself again. Stacie promotes believing that obstacles in life are not the end but a new beginning where the old dies and the new emerges into amazing opportunities.

The first time writing about her story publicly since blindness in 2016, while her faith wavered at the beginning of her blindness, was also her faith that strengthened her resolve to be better and provide a voice for others who need an extra hand or support. Also, Stacie has served in many volunteer positions within the National Federation of the Blind.

Stacy dedicates her chapter, "Leap of Faith," to God and her daughter Alana. In the future, she aspires to write a memoir of her journey overcoming physical abuse, blindness, and being a single parent.

Daria Bannerman

My name is Daria Bannerman. I was born in a small town called Maple Hill in North Carolina, a town filled with community and good-natured people. In my thirty-two years of life, God has allowed me to accomplish many things. I graduated valedictorian in 2008, received my Bachelor of Arts in English degree in 2013, and obtained my Master of Social Work degree in 2017.

I was able to help an awesome organization give blankets, words of encouragement, and other needed items to families whose children are experiencing illness at the Ronald McDonald House in Maryland. I was able to help this same organization raise funds for the National Federation of the Blind, its proceeds going toward white canes and scholarships for those who are blind/visually impaired. Advocating for people with disabilities has been a passion of mine for years. I was able to accomplish all these feats because I trusted and relied on the Lord. Were there times I wanted to give up? Yes. Did I sometimes doubt my ability to make a difference in this world? Definitely. However, I sought the Lord during difficult times. I even started picking up the Bible and reading His Word and realizing His promises and His love for me. As a result, I can share and demonstrate His love with whoever I have encountered. This chapter is an example of the challenges I have faced and what I had to do to navigate and overcome them. I hope and pray that this chapter encourages and uplifts you as you read these heartfelt words.

Kamille Richardson

Kamille Richardson is the founder of iSee Technologies. Her company teaches people who are blind and visually impaired how to use assistive technology in order to gain independence and connect with the world.

She also provides education and consultation to corporate entities and multiple organizations on the importance of diversity and inclusion for the blind and visually impaired in the employment space as well as from the customer perspective.

Kamille has been totally blind from birth. Her trials and triumphs throughout her life's journey fuel her passion to give voice to an often overlooked demographic. When she is not educating and motivating, you can find her at the nearest beach with her family and friends or binging the latest Netflix drama.

Krystle Allen

Krystle Allen is a Newark, New Jersey native. She is a millennial entrepreneur and non-profiteer who is no stranger to community development, social change, and grassroots efforts. She is presently employed with the New Jersey Commission for the Blind and Visually Impaired under the Department of Human Services in the role of the community outreach specialist.

Simultaneously, Krystle serves as the founder and president of a growing non-profit organization in the city of Newark called Eyes Like Mine Inc. Her mission is to share awareness about the abilities and potential of individuals with vision loss through community service initiatives, comprehensive empowerment workshops, and innovative social change awareness events.

With dazzle and bling, her personality shines throughout her chapter, “Me Time: Affirming The Shape of My Collage of Healing.” Not knowing her sight lost would become her vision gained.

Cheryl Minnette

Surprisingly, going from sighted to sight lost increased Cheryl Minnette's skillset. She is an international motivational speaker, best-selling author, writer, and creator/host of The Cooking Blind Kitchen. Cheryl is a visionary strategist who repositions your life's direction.

Cheryl assists women to boldly step into their forefront to ignite their passions and growth. She understands the power one's mind holds and how using it can transform you into your best self. Cheryl has been named "Woman on the Move" by *Bold Blind Beauty Magazine* and honored by Women Thriving Fearlessly. Learn more by contacting Cheryl at cherylspeakslife@gmail.com.

Mirranda Williams

Mirranda Williams is a first-time author participating in the *Write 2 Heal* anthology. She identifies herself as an original Georgia peach that has been transplanted to the soil of Maryland. She believes that the historical black leaders' blood, sweat, and tears that watered the soil of Baltimore has played a key role and provided her with the much-needed nourishment to bring forth her sweetest self!

Although her favorite genre to read is historical romances, her work is non-fictional because she desires to plant a seed in her readers through the writing of her life's journey to help others recognize that owning their truth is the only way to begin to heal. As a current graduate student at Morgan State University, Mirranda is committed to pursuing a career as a practitioner within the field of social work with a specialization in Gerontology. She has a zeal for advocacy and empowerment work for the differently abled population. She looks forward to helping the aging community with an emphasis on blindness and low vision once she completes her matriculation. Until that moment comes, she endeavors to write in hopes that her stories will be the catalyst for her readers in understanding that they too have the *Write 2 Heal!*

Made in the USA
Middletown, DE
01 June 2022

66535406R00099